EVERGREEN PILOT BOOKS

Chief Editor
A. Norman Jeffares

Advisory Editors
David Daiches   C. P. Snow

EDWIN MUIR

EDWIN MUIR

P. H. Butter

GROVE PRESS, INC.
NEW YORK

First published by Oliver & Boyd Ltd
Edinburgh, Scotland, 1962

Library of Congress Catalog Card Number: 61-12359

First Evergreen Edition 1962

Manufactured in Great Britain

CONTENTS

ACKNOWLEDGMENTS

I am grateful to Mrs Muir for permission to use a microfilm of manuscripts, and for other help, as well as for permission to quote from her husband's works; to Mrs Ross and Mrs Abenheimer (Muir's nieces) for permission to use letters to their mother and father; to Mrs McIntyre and Mr W. D. Ritchie for communicating reminiscences of Muir; and to two American scholars, Mr Elgin Mellown and Mr Robert Hollander, for helpful answers to queries, and to the latter for permission to use material from his Columbia University D.Phil. thesis *A Textual and Bibliographical Study of the Poems of Edwin Muir*.

Acknowledgments are due to the following publishers for permission to quote from the works of Edwin Muir indicated: Allen and Unwin Ltd and Alfred A. Knopf Inc. (*We Moderns*); Jonathan Cape Ltd (*John Knox*); Cresset Press and The McBride Co. (*The Present Age*); J. M. Dent and Sons Ltd (*Journeys and Places*); Faber and Faber Ltd and Grove Press Inc. (*Collected Poems 1921–1958*); George Harrap and Co. Ltd (*The Story and the Fable*); William Heinemann Ltd (*Scottish Journey*); Hogarth Press Ltd (*An Autobiography, Chorus of the Newly Dead, Essays on Literature and Society, The Marionette, The Structure of the Novel, Transition*); William Sloane Associates, Inc. (*An Autobiography*); Routledge and Kegan Paul Ltd (*Scott and Scotland*); Viking Press Inc. (*John Knox, The Marionette, Transition*).

Acknowledgments are also due to the following for permission to quote from the works indicated: *The Hudson Review* (art. by John Holloway); Sidgwick and Jackson Ltd (*The Modern Poet*, ed. Gwendolen Murphy.)

The photograph on the front cover is reproduced by permission of *The Glasgow Herald*.

P. B.

ABBREVIATED TITLES
BY WHICH MUIR'S WORKS
ARE CITED IN REFERENCES

A.	=	*An Autobiography*
C.N.D.	=	*Chorus of the newly Dead*
C.P.	=	*Collected Poems: 1921–58*
K.	=	*John Knox: Portrait of a Calvinist*
L.	=	*Latitudes*
L.S.	=	*Essays on Literature and Society*
M.	=	*The Marionette*
P.A.	=	*The Present Age*
S.F.	=	*The Story and the Fable*
S.J.	=	*Scottish Journey*
S.N.	=	*The Structure of the Novel*
S.S.	=	*Scott and Scotland*
T.	=	*Transition*
W.M.	=	*We Moderns*

CHAPTER I

THE MAN

Edwin Muir spoke in a soft and gentle voice, which was difficult to hear in a noisy room. His works, too, only gradually made themselves heard above more assertive voices. He followed no fashions, made no startling innovations in technique, never sought popularity by surface brilliance. But now that time is wearing away the slick, the crude, and the merely modish from the poetry of the last forty years, the beauty of his later poems and the wisdom they contain are coming to be more widely appreciated. These poems need to be lived with and long meditated over; they grow in the mind as one gets to know them better, whereas some more immediately exciting ones shrink. It is a help to know something of the experience that went into them; so a good way to approach them is by way of his *Autobiography*.

He was born in 1887 on a farm on a small island in the Orkneys. In describing his childhood there he does not conceal the darker side—the exactions of the landlord, the fears, the sense of guilt which oppressed him for a time, his dislike of school—but stresses mainly the good things which were later lost. The main features of his childhood experience as he later reconstructed it were a sense of unity, of timelessness and of splendour. Unity first in a united family in a home which was a place of security, an order. His father and mother were kindly and religious people, and he could not remember "ever hearing them exchanging a discourteous word or raising their voices to each other."[1] The worst punishment the children knew was "an occasional clip across the ears

from my father's soft cap. . . . Afterwards he would sit
back looking ashamed."[2] The family consisted of four
brothers, of whom Edwin was the youngest, and two
sisters, and they had a cousin and an aunt living with
them. Living in that remote place they made their own
entertainment. The father was a fine story-teller, the
mother a singer, the two eldest brothers played the
fiddle, and they were all expert on the melodeon:

> The winter gathered us into one room as it gathered
> the cattle into the stable and the byre; the sky came
> closer; the lamps were lit at three or four in the after-
> noon, and then the great evening lay before us like a
> world: an evening filled with talk, stories, games,
> music, and lamplight.[3]

Sunday was a special night, when the father

> gathered us together to read a chapter of the Bible
> and kneel down in prayer. These Sunday nights are
> among my happiest memories; there was a feeling of
> complete security and union among us as we sat
> reading about David or Elijah. My father's prayer,
> delivered in a sort of mild chant while we knelt on the
> floor, generally ran on the same lines; at one point
> there always came the words, for which I waited,
> "an house not made with hands, eternal in the
> heavens".[4]

Second, around this ordered and united home was
an ordered, non-competitive community, untouched by
industrialism:

> The farmers did not know ambition and the petty
> torments of ambition; they did not realize what
> competition was, though they lived at the end of
> Queen Victoria's reign; they helped one another with
> their work when help was required, following the old
> usage; they had a culture made up of legend, folk-

song and the poetry and prose of the Bible; they had customs which sanctioned their instinctive feelings for the earth; their life was an order, and a good order.[5]

Third, the child had a sense of a yet larger unity—a sense of oneness with the natural life around him. The horses on the farm, the insects, the grass, even the inanimate things seemed to have a life of their own—mysterious, sometimes terrifying, but bound to the life of men:

A child has ... a picture of human existence peculiar to himself, which he probably never remembers after he has lost it: the original vision of the world. I think of this picture or vision as that of a state in which the earth, the houses on the earth, and the life of every human being are related to the sky overarching them; as if the sky fitted the earth and the earth the sky. Certain dreams convince me that a child has this vision, in which there is a completer harmony of all things with each other than he will ever know again.[6]

There was nothing sentimental about this. He does not fail to mention the harsher side of things—the storms which caused wrecks on the dangerous coast, the killings of animals on the farm, his fear of as well as delight in the horses, his loathing of some insects. But, whether loathsome or terrifying or splendid, all things seemed to share a common life.

Allied to this sense of unity and order was a sense of timelessness. There is a time in early childhood before we become conscious that time moves and that all things change. In later life we know people first as strangers, as separate people all following the laws of their different natures. But our father and mother were never strangers to us, nor our brothers and sisters if we were the last born, as Muir was. They seemed to him then to have been always there, and he with them, since he could not account for himself; at the same time his brothers and sisters were to him new creatures, existing not in time but in a vast, boundless calm. . . . That world was a perfectly solid world, for the days did not undermine it but merely rounded it, or rather repeated it, as if there were only one day endlessly rising and setting. Our first childhood is the only time in our lives when we exist within immortality, and perhaps all our ideas of immortality are influenced by it.[7]

His later writings on immortality were controlled by this experience. He always treated it not primarily as a belief, but as a state of being, a mode of apprehension. In early childhood we unconsciously exist within immortality; later we can in dreams and in certain special moments return to this state of being and consciously apprehend its significance.

The other chief quality of his childhood vision was an apprehension of what Wordsworth called a "splendour in the objects of sense." He remembered later the suit in which he was baptised at the age of three. It was scarlet with gold buttons, and "the cloth seemed to glow from within with its own light." It was the suit that made him remember that day, and "it still burns in my memory more brightly than anything I have ever seen since."[8]

A sense of unity, of timelessness, of splendour—these were the main characteristics of his childhood Eden, a state recovered later occasionally in dreams and moments of memory. A similar innocence of vision has been described in similar terms by others—Traherne, Blake, Wordsworth spring to mind—but by none more convincingly. Muir's quiet tone and uninflated prose assure us of his integrity. He was well aware of the possibility of reading back into the past later feelings and insights. In describing how he saw a pig rather inefficiently killed in the farm-yard he wrote: "Later, in memory, it seemed to me that I had pitied the pig; but I know that I did not; my terror was too great, and what I felt for it was hatred, for the pig seemed formidable and evil."[9] Of course, the experience as recollected by the mature man is inevitably to some degree different from the child's experience. It is a sort of fusion of past and present, and it is, perhaps, this fusion that gives the sense of timelessness. To recover early innocence and to combine it with later experience in a new whole was a large part of Muir's effort as a poet.

The journey out of Eden began at the age of six with the onset of a consciousness of change, of death, and of guilt. At about this time a neighbouring farmer, who had been kind to him, died in great pain, and he himself had a sharp attack of influenza. Soon afterwards he passed through a phase of acute childish guilt, associated with a sack of sheep-dip which his father had warned the children not to touch because it was poisonous. After the dip had been used he felt that he could not be sure that he had not touched the sack. "My fear was beyond any argument, so I washed my hands many times a day until they had a wasted transparent look, and pored upon them afterwards in a sort of agony."[10] He seemed to himself isolated in a world of guilt and fear, divided from the rest of the family who were still in the ordinary world. The phase passed, but the earlier state was never quite recovered. He was at first unhappy at school, being shy and at times unwell.

When he was eight the family moved to a farm near Kirkwall. The land was poor, the house damp. The family began to break up, his brothers and sisters leaving one by one to take jobs in Kirkwall, Glasgow, and Edinburgh. His mother was often ill, and his father strained his heart in the effort to keep the farm going. He himself went, rather irregularly, to school in Kirkwall. He was beginning self-consciously to try to grow up. "I had lost my first clear vision of the world, and reached the stage when a child tries desperately to see things as his elders see them, and hopes to grow up by pretending to be grown up."[11] It was an inevitable process of adjustment, the putting on of a mask, the preparing of a "face to meet the faces that you meet." After a time he found himself able to get on with the other boys at school, of whom he had at first been afraid—but only at the cost of some falsification, some suppression of individuality, a self-coarsening to meet the coarseness of others. He had lost his "first delight in things; life had a purpose and had grown drier."[12] The main gain of those years was that he began to read avidly.

At fourteen he went to a revivalist meeting, and, caught up by the emotional fervour of the gathering, experienced a "conversion"—of a rather dubious kind, but one, nevertheless, which had real, though passing, effects on him. A sort of purification took place in him, and washed away the poisonous stuff that had gathered in the past year. But, he later thought, it would be ridiculous to call this a genuine religious conversion. He did not know what he was doing, had no clear knowledge of sin nor of the need of salvation.

The next long step out of Eden came when the family moved to Glasgow when he was still fourteen. It was a sudden transition from a mainly agricultural, traditional, co-operative community to the fiercely competitive life of a great industrial city. This move brought great misfortunes to the family, but it is worth stressing that Muir's journey out of Eden had begun long before. This journey he presents as an inevitable part of growing up, not as a result of the move. He did regard the life he had known in Orkney as superior to that which he later saw in Glasgow, but was not so simple-minded as to suppose that small farmers live in a state of sinlessness, or that people in large towns are necessarily inferior to them.

In Glasgow thousands lived in the squalor of some of the worst slums in Europe; above them the more prosperous working class and the lower middle class were fearfully conscious of the abyss into which some misfortune might throw them; for the thrustful and the lucky there were chances to fight their way up to a life in which they would try desperately to insulate their minds, their hearts and their senses from a full realization of the misery around them. Muir was never among the very poor, though his work as an office-boy at first brought in only 4s. 2d. a week; he was never a slum-dweller, though for years he walked through the slums every day on his way to and from work:

These journeys filled me with a sense of degradation: the crumbling houses, the twisted faces, the obscene words heard casually in passing, the ancient, haunting stench of pollution and decay, the arrogant women, the mean men, the terrible children, daunted me, and at last filled me with an immense, blind dejection.[13]

After a time he taught himself not to see, to get used to these things; but when he was tired or ill the horror would return, and "the slums seemed to be everywhere around me, a great, spreading swamp into which I might sink for good."[14]

His father especially found it difficult to adjust himself to the new life—to such things as the need to shut the door of their flat when going out, to the necessity of turning away beggars, to being dependent on money rather than on things he could produce; before long he died suddenly of a heart attack. A year after this, when Muir was sixteen, his elder brother Willie died of consumption after a slow, painful illness. He himself became ill, lost his job, and was advised to look for open-air work. This led to a comparatively happy interlude of a few months as an apprentice chauffeur on an estate in Ayrshire. Returning to Glasgow he found another elder brother, Johnnie, dying in an even more painful and gradual way than Willie had done; he had a tumour on the brain, which affected his mind and his power to control his limbs. The brothers walked out together on fine summer evenings, sometimes watching football or cricket. For a few moments Johnnie would forget his illness, but the contrast between his own lumbering gait and the careless ease of others soon brought it back to him. He retreated into himself, and the brothers walked on through the cheerful crowded streets, paying no attention to others, "as detached and cold as monks."[15] Every night Muir prayed that his brother would get better, but the pain only increased. If Johnnie could have recovered and become a new man, purged by suffering, there might have been some meaning in his agony. "But, if he had to die in any case, what point could there be, I asked myself night after night, in that impersonal, systematic torture which as it went on wrecked in turn his body, his mind, and his spirit . . . ? I could find no answer to that question, except that life was ruled by an iron law."[16] Johnnie died after great agony, to be followed soon by his mother. In his works, right up to the late poem, *The Brothers*, Muir shows himself much preoccupied with the relationship of brothers. It seems that the differing temperaments of the three brothers led to quarrels ("In life I and my brothers fought" is a cancelled line in the working-out of the poem), but that they were strongly attached to each other. If there had been tensions, this would probably make the deaths of Willie and Johnnie all the more painful for Muir. These early years in Glasgow were the worst in his life.

He was now nineteen. The remaining members of the family were grown up, and went their separate ways. Muir stayed on in Glasgow, in lodgings, earning 16s. a week in a cheerful office of a beer-bottling factory. He made friends with other intelligent young people with whom he could discuss literature and politics. He became a socialist, a member of the Clarion Scouts and later of the I.L.P. His conversion to socialism was parallel to his earlier religious conversion at Kirkwall. "It was not . . . the result of an intellectual process, but rather a process of emotional transmutation; the poisonous stuff which had gathered in me during the past few years had found another temporary discharge."[17] The world around, and people, were transformed because he could look at them with hope, could see them as they might become in a better society. His religious faith, already weakened by the deaths of his brothers, was submerged beneath this new, purely secular, ideal. His state of exaltation did not last long, but his work for socialism continued to give his life hope and purpose, and to bring him into association with other like-minded people.

In his early twenties he found stimulating company in a group of the Clarion Scouts known as "the intellectuals." They went for country walks, and discussed everything—biology, history, sex, comparative religion, even theology—and followed the literary and intellectual developments of the time, discovering Bergson, Conrad, Forster, Joyce, Lawrence, etc. Muir took A. R. Orage's periodical, *The New Age*. This was a highbrow weekly, dealing with politics (supporting Guild Socialism and later Social Credit), philosophy, and the arts. It included skits and parodies, and exposés of social injustices and of cant and humbug in the pronouncements of prominent persons. Its tone was "crushingly superior and exclusive."[18] It was stimulating for the young Muir and made him feel in touch with the latest developments in thought and the arts, but it encouraged him to assume attitudes and opinions that were not really native to him. This was a time of intellectual experimentation and widening interests, a more hopeful period than the earlier years in Glasgow; but his personal circumstances were still unpromising. He was still only a poor clerk, with little prospect of becoming anything else. Looking around at elderly clerks, become round-backed and grey at their work, he was sometimes overcome by dejection. Having been advised by Orage to take up some one writer and study all his work, he chose Nietzsche, and, in compensation for the narrowness of his life and prospects, took refuge in the fantasy of a Superman. His Nietzscheanism and his socialism were, of course, incompatible; but he would not allow himself to recognise this.

When he was about twenty-five the beer-bottling business was taken over by a new owner, and he found a new job in a bone-factory at Fairport, a small town on the sea not far from Glasgow. There for two years he experienced new depths of industrial squalor. Bones, covered with maggots, were brought from all over Scotland, shovelled into furnaces, and reduced to charcoal and grease. The factory, and sometimes most of the town, were enveloped in stench. "It was a gentle, clinging, sweet stench, suggesting dissolution and hospitals and slaughter-houses, the odour of drains, and the rancid stink of bad, roasting meat."[19] Added to the physical squalor was a feeling of moral degradation. The office at Fairport had been badly conducted, and was constantly under fire from the clean and methodical head office in Glasgow. Muir had to find excuses for the errors made by others and "drearily lie them away every day, year in, year out. I ended by acquiring a habitual bad conscience, a constant expectation of being accused."[20] A nervous stomach trouble, from which he had suffered earlier, returned, and he was physically and spiritually in a bad way. Fortunately, soon after the outbreak of war, a friend got him a job back in Glasgow. He offered himself for the Army, but was refused on medical grounds, and continued to work throughout the War in a ship-building office. Life was in some ways better than it had been at Fairport. He took an interest in Guild Socialism; had intelligent friends, including Francis George Scott, the composer, and Denis Saurat; and began to write for *The New Age*. But he was lonely and unhappy, not far indeed from nervous collapse. At thirty he had travelled far from his early Eden. Instead of the feeling of unity and splendour was a sense of division—both within himself and from things outside. Sometimes he would waken with a start from a reverie, conscious that for some time he had been staring at some chance object. It was as if he could grasp what was before his eyes only by an enormous effort, and even then an invisible barrier separated him from it. "I moved in a crystalline globe or bubble, insulated from the life around me, yet filled with desire to reach it, to be at the very heart of it and to lose myself there."[21] In some moods things seemed as much alive as they had done in the early days, but now they seemed hostile, not related to him nor to human life in any harmonious order:

A jagged stone or a thistle seemed to be bursting with malice, as if they had been put into the world to cut and gash; the dashing of breakers on rocks terrified me, for I was both the wave and the rock; it was as though I were both too close to things and immeasurably distant from them.[22]

He sought refuge from his inner conflicts in company, and was both more sociable and more lonely than ever before. At this point his own account, which lays most stress on his inner life, needs to be supplemented by the memories of others. Mr W. D. Ritchie, an associate in the Guild Socialist movement, remembers him as an "angry young man," bitter, argumentative, a voluble talker when roused. Mrs McIntyre (then Jessie Roberton, daughter of Sir Hugh Roberton, conductor of the Orpheus Choir) remembers him as a delightful companion, a very good dancer, an entertaining talker with a great width and variety of knowledge of the arts. He was, however, she says, unsure of himself, both in personal relationships (he had an idea he would never marry) and with regard to his prospects as a writer. Both were conscious of great gifts in him, which were being wasted in his life as a clerk. The delightful companion, the voluble Guildsman, the Nietzschean who was writing aphorisms for *The New Age*, were all aspects of himself, as well as the unhappy young man revealed in the *Autobiography*. But to some extent he was wearing masks, adopting attitudes that were not native to him. He was not a whole personality. He might never have become so, might never have achieved the work of which he was capable, if he had not in 1918 met Willa Anderson. Next year they were married, and without a job between them and with very little money went to London. "If my wife had not encouraged me it is unlikely that I should ever have taken the plunge myself; I was still paralysed by my inward conflict. My marriage was the most fortunate event in my life."[23] It was indeed so. He especially needed some one with her great courage to help him.

This was the turning-point in his life, the beginning of the journey back to the lost Eden, a journey which is to be followed in his poetry rather than in the record of the external events of his life. In London he became assistant to Orage on *The New Age*, and got other literary work. But the Glasgow years left their aftermath. He was still troubled with irrational fears. He underwent a course of psycho-analysis, which was at first very painful. Material from the unconscious gushed up in dreams and day-dreams, some of which he recorded and used later in his poetry. After a time he was advised by the analyst to stop the waking dreams, which he was able to do. Though nervously exhausting, these experiences helped him to face, and so release himself from, past conflicts. He freed himself from his Nietzscheanism, and recovered his faith in immortality.

In the summer of 1921 he and his wife went abroad for four years—to Prague, to Dresden and nearby Hellerau, to Italy in the summer of 1923, and finally to Austria. This was the most leisured and peaceful period of his adult life. He wrote articles for *The New Age* and for an American periodical, *The Freeman*, but was less under pressure than he was later to be. They were able to live quite cheaply. After *The Freeman* ceased publication in 1924 they began to translate from the German. Thanks to this peace and to the influence of his wife he seemed at last at Dresden to recover from the long illness which had seized him when, at fourteen, he had gone to Glasgow. He felt the need to go back again over the years he had lived wrongly, and in doing so came to know himself for the first time. Looking back over his own life he saw it not only as the unique story of one man, but as a fable related to the lives of other men and of the race; for "the life of every man is an endlessly repeated performance of the life of man."[24] In recovering past time he released himself, in a measure from time:

> In turning my head and looking *against* the direction in which time was hurrying me I won a new kind of experience; for now that I no longer marched in step with time I could see life timelessly, and with that in terms of the imagination. I felt, though I had not the ability to express it, what Proust describes in *Le Temps retrouvé*. "A moment liberated from the order of time" seemed actually to have re-created in me "a man to feel it who was also freed from the order of time". But as this kind of looking required the use of imagination it wakened my imagination, sluggishly at first.[25]

This awakening led him, at the age of thirty-five, to begin to write poetry—the proper means of expression for this new imaginative vision.

He had now found his true *métier* as a poet, but years of practising his art were needed before he was to be able to express his distinctive vision with full power. The conditions of his life were not to give him much leisure to practise his proper vocation. He and his wife returned to England in 1925, and lived there—except for a two-year interval in the South of France, some visits to P.E.N. conferences abroad and to Scotland—for the next ten years, until 1932 in the country and then for three years in Hampstead. In 1927 their son Gavin was born. It was a great struggle to make their living as free-lance writers.

Their main bread-and-butter resource was translating from the German. In addition he wrote many articles for periodicals and a large number of reviews. All this work was done with great conscientiousness. He would not undertake any work, however lucrative, that would prevent him being true to his standards. Lord Beaverbrook, impressed by his biography of John Knox, offered him work in 1929, but he refused it. (After his interview with Beaverbrook he wrote to his sister, Mrs Thorburn: "I rather liked the old rascal.") When one remembers all this and the fact that they, especially Mrs Muir, were at times hampered by ill health, one wonders that they managed to produce so much original, creative work. Between 1925 and 1935 he published three volumes of poetry, three novels, three books of criticism, a biography of Knox, and *Scottish Journey*. She published two novels, *Imagined Corners* and *Mrs Ritchie*, which deserve, especially the second, more attention than they have received.

In their first English home, in Buckinghamshire, they were befriended by Sidney Schiff ("Stephen Hudson," the novelist), whose circle, including the Muirs, is maliciously described by Wyndham Lewis in *Apes of God*, PT IX. But they did not have a very busy social life until they moved to Hampstead. Several other writers were living near them there, and they had many friends. Though not yet famous, he was already much admired and liked by those who knew him—for his integrity, his fair-mindedness, his absence of self-seeking as well as for his intelligence and wit. Though his energies were fully taken up by his writing, he was still greatly concerned about social and political matters. He had written to his sister and brother-in-law from the South of France in the year of the General Strike that "it is unbearable sometimes to look on and do nothing." Some of his Hampstead friends believed that hope for the future lay in Communism, but Communism seemed to him an inhuman system. Characteristically, one of his chief objections to it was that it finds no place for forgiveness, "no chink through which mercy to a bad or lapsed Communist can steal, or admiration for a brave or good opponent. The religious man is bound to forgive; the ordinary man forgives easily. Without forgiveness our life would be unimaginable. ...."[26] Communism seemed to him to display in more extreme form all that he had most disliked in Calvinism.[27] Influenced by his old mentor, A. R. Orage, who had come back to England in 1932 after ten years in America and had started *The New English Weekly*, he embraced Social Credit as the most hopeful means of achieving the transition to a new society without violence. He was concerned about international as well as home politics, and started in 1934 with Janko Lavrin a new periodical, *The European Quarterly*, intended "to foster the growth of the European spirit in every sphere of human activity." This quarterly contained writing of very high quality, but did not last long.

In spite of these public anxieties the years in Hampstead were happy ones. They came to an end as a result of Gavin Muir, then five, being run over by an oil tanker; his broken leg healed, but he remained very nervous of traffic, and his parents decided to move to a quieter place. In 1935, after a month in Orkney, they settled in St Andrews. They did not have so many friends there as they had had in Hampstead; Scotland did not give him the recognition that he deserved. It was not, however, primarily for these reasons that Muir went through times of acute depression at St Andrews. He was now middle-aged, and felt that he had not achieved what he was capable of. The necessity to go on translating German books for a living was burdensome. He had written very little poetry with which he was satisfied. He seemed to himself to be living a trivial, routine life, doing literary hack-work while being conscious in himself of imaginative powers which he was not able to make full use of. In addition he shared to the full the general anxieties over industrial depression at home and the worsening situation in Europe. He was closer to these things than many of the more directly "committed" writers of the thirties; they hit him in personal ways. His brother-in-law, George Thorburn, had been one of those thrown out of work by the industrial depression, and he had done what he could to help the family. Now the advances of Nazi Germany into Austria and then Czechoslovakia engulfed or drove into exile many friends and acquaintances.

All this time, beneath the surface, his spiritual pilgrimage was going on. His marriage, his psycho-analysis, his recovery of a sense of immortality, the awakening of his imagination had been steps on the way. But he had not yet reached any secure faith. At times he had intuitions of freedom and eternity, but at other times he felt that men, himself included, were no more than animals imprisoned within time in an iron chain of cause and effect. A renewal of faith and the inner strength to confront the external anxieties came early in 1939. When walking home from visiting his wife who was recovering from an illness he saw children playing marbles on the pavement; "the old game had 'come round' again at its own time, known only to children, and it seemed a simple little rehearsal for a resurrection, promising a timeless renewal of life." That night, undressing for bed, he found himself "reciting the Lord's Prayer in a loud, emphatic voice—a thing I had not done for many years—with deep urgency and profound disturbed emotion." He became calmer, and as he repeated the prayer over and over "meaning after meaning sprang from it, overcoming me with joyful surprise; and I realized that this simple petition was always universal and always inexhaustible, and day by day sanctified human life." For many years he had clung to belief in God and the immortality of the soul, even though at times tempted to despair; now he realised that he was a Christian, "no matter how bad a one," and had a sense "that Christ was the turning-point of time and the meaning of life to everyone, no matter what his conscious beliefs."[28] This was a conversion of a far more profound and lasting nature than his earlier ones in Kirkwall and Glasgow. It was the result not of momentary emotion nor of external stimulus, but of years of patient effort to find the right road and follow it. It was this new-found faith, together with his increasing mastery of his art, which enabled him to achieve the marvellous flowering of his poetry in the years to come.

Externally, however, life continued to be a struggle. War stopped his income from German translations, and his other work did not bring in enough to keep the home going. Mrs Muir got work as a teacher, and he a job in the Food Office in Dundee; but illness (in Mrs Muir's case a very severe one, of which she nearly died) prevented them from continuing with these jobs for long. Fortunately, early in 1942, he was offered work by the British Council in Edinburgh for which he was excellently qualified—arranging evening programmes of lectures, concerts, etc., for international houses set up there for soldiers and refugees from Poland, Czechoslovakia, and other countries. In Edinburgh he was busy and among friends, and wrote more poetry than in all his time in St Andrews. What was in him was at last beginning to find adequate expression.

After the War, in 1945, he was sent by the British Council to Prague as Director of the Institute there. He enjoyed making contact again with the Czechs, seeing places where he had been happy twenty-five years before, and teaching the hard-working students at Charles University; but the history he saw being made was tragic. Between the German occupation and the Communist coup of 1948 the Czechs enjoyed but a brief and anxious spell of freedom. After the coup he found that he could no longer make any real contact with his students, and asked to be transferred to another post. After his return to England a feeling of blankness and desolation, occasioned by what he had seen, settled on him for a time.

In 1949 he was sent to Rome as Director of the British Council Institute. His eighteen months there amid the artistic glories of the city and the gaiety and friendliness of its people were happy ones. In St Andrews ten years earlier he had come to a realisation of his Christian faith, but had not turned to any Church nor had any conception of the splendours of Christendom. In his childhood he had been "aware of religion chiefly as the sacred Word," and the bare Presbyterian churches had seemed "to cut off religion from the rest of life and from all the week-day world. . . . Nothing told me that Christ was born in the flesh and had lived on the earth."[29] But in Rome the image of the Incarnation was to be seen everywhere, not only in churches, but in houses, in wayside shrines in the parks and at cross-roads in the suburbs. "This open declaration was to me the very mark of Christianity, distinguishing it from the older religions. For although the pagan gods had visited the earth and conversed with men, they did not assume the burden of our flesh, live our life and die our death."[30] This was the end of his spiritual pilgrimage, the answer to the question he had been trying to work out in his poetry of the relation between time and eternity.

In 1950 he returned to Scotland to become Warden of Newbattle Abbey College near Edinburgh. Here came adult students—clerks, fitters, turners, tube-makers, railwaymen, etc.—whose circumstances had prevented them from pursuing academic studies earlier, such people as Muir himself had been in his Glasgow years. They came usually for a year; some returned afterwards to their previous work, others went on to university. "They were eager, and more intelligent than I had ever dreamed they could be, and to watch over them and see their minds unfolding was an experience I am glad not to have

missed."[31] Muir was an inspiring teacher, and was regarded with great affection and devotion by those of his
staff and students who were capable of appreciating him;
but he was not so well suited to the administrative and
committee work and did not receive from the authorities
all the help to which he was entitled. He retired in 1955,
went to America to Harvard for a year, and then returned to settle in a pleasant village near Cambridge.
He was now nearly seventy and rather frail in health,
but the quality of the poetry he was writing was as high
as ever, though he was not even now able to devote all
his remaining energy to it. His work, though quite in-
valuable, had not been financially very profitable, and
he was concerned about the future of his wife and son.
Almost to the end (he died in January 1959) he continued
to review for the *Observer*. If he had been financially
secure the harvest of his last years might have been
greater in quantity.

But he would not wish any account of his life to end on
a note of complaint. Though his acute sensitivity, especially to other people's distresses, made him vulnerable,
one thinks of him as anything but a gloomy person. In
some slight Christmastide verses sent to friends in 1953
he and his wife gave as reasons for their feeling rather
exhausted after very full lives that "in the past we have
worked hard and over-much laughed." Those who knew
him in his last years, even slightly, were greatly impressed by his serenity, his integrity, his wisdom, his
unfailing kindness to all who sought his help, especially
to young writers, and, perhaps above all, his humility.
One felt beneath the gentle, unassertive surface the
presence of a richer, intenser life, and a profounder
vision than any but a very few ever attain to. He had
not had an easy life. In Glasgow he had endured the
sight of the painful deaths of his two brothers and of the
degradation of the slums, and had spent eighteen years
in dull routine work much beneath his powers; later he

had been near mental breakdown and had gone through
other periods of acute depression; he had never been
financially secure, and had had to spend much of his
energy, which could have been better used, on translating and reviewing. But in many ways it had been a
good life for a poet. He had experienced widely as well
as deeply, and had touched life at many points. In
childhood he had known an ancient, pre-industrial
civilisation in Orkney; later he had experienced, more
from the inside than most literary men, industrial life at
its worst in Glasgow, and then had known the cultural
life of some of the great cities of Europe. He had become,
to a greater extent than most British literary men of his
time, a European, knowing—not only from literature,
but from personal contacts—the cultures of several
countries. Though from 1919 a man of letters he had not
lived in a literary ivory tower, but had been deeply concerned about the political and social situation in his own
country and in Europe. As a teacher in his later years he
had kept in touch with the young, and with people from
different social and national backgrounds. He had enjoyed a happy marriage. All these experiences entered
into his later poetry, and helped to give it breadth. But
these many interests did not—as the day-to-day concerns
of most of us tend to do—suppress his deeper, visionary,
imaginative self. Like Wordsworth he was able to return
in manhood to the hiding places of his power in the past,
and, unlike Wordsworth, he was able to keep the channel
open right into old age. Delving beneath the surface of
his own life he was able to see it as a fable, related to the
lives of others and to that of the race, and so to illuminate
the experience of others for them. He had known Eden,
the Fall, the journey through the labyrinth of time and
the journey back to the recovery of an innocence which
could be combined with experience.

On his tombstone are, appropriately, carved the words
from his poem, *Milton*:

his unblinded eyes
Saw far and near the fields of Paradise.

Even in this life, where vision is limited, he himself had
been able to see something of Paradise not only far, but
also near, not only in memories of childhood and in
literature, but also in the adult and every-day world. And
so, looking back over a life whose sufferings might have
embittered many, his last words on it were of gratitude:

As I look back on the part of the mystery which is my
own life, my own fable, what I am most aware of is that
we receive more than we can ever give; we receive it
from the past, on which we draw with every breath,
but also—and this is a point of faith—from the Source
of the mystery itself, by the means which religious
people call Grace.[32]

REFERENCES

1. *A.*, p. 27.
2. *A.*, p. 27.
3. *A.*, pp. 30–1.
4. *A.*, p. 26.
5. *A.*, p. 63.
6. *A.*, p. 33.
7. *A.*, p. 25.
8. *A.*, p. 18.
9. *A.*, p. 37.
10. *A.*, p. 34.
11. *A.*, p. 66.
12. *A.*, p. 71.
13. *A.*, pp. 91–2.
14. *A.*, p. 92.
15. *A.*, p. 102.
16. *A.*, p. 103.
17. *A.*, p. 113.
18. *A.*, p. 123.
19. *A.*, p. 131.
20. *A.*, p. 133.
21. *A.*, pp. 149–50.
22. *A.*, p. 150.
23. *A.*, p. 154.
24. *A.*, p. 49.
25. *A.*, p. 193.
26. *A.*, p. 235.
27. See his article "Bolshevism
    and Calvinism," in *The
    New English Weekly*, 21
    Jun. 1934.
28. *A.*, pp. 246–7.
29. *A.*, pp. 277–8.
30. *A.*, p. 278.
31. *A.*, p. 279.
32. *A.*, p. 281.

CHAPTER II

THE CRITIC:
OF LITERATURE AND SOCIETY

Much of Muir's prose is very interesting and well-written, though it is not of the same permanent importance as the poetry. It will be useful to look at the prose first in order to see the range of his ideas and interests.

He made his living for most of his life as a busy translator and critic. He and his wife produced forty-three volumes of translations, mostly from German. They performed an important service in making Kafka and Hermann Broch known to English readers. I am told by a German scholar that the Kafka translations not only are accurate, but also convey something of the flavour of the original. Not all the books they translated, however, were worth the time and energy they had to spend on them. His periodical writings comprise about a thousand reviews and something like three hundred articles, etc. He was a very fair reviewer, always looking for something in a book which he could sincerely praise; he would refuse to write about a book in which he could find nothing good. He was quick to see outstanding merit, and wrote with enthusiasm of Patrick White long before he was widely known; in 1942 he wrote of his *Happy Valley* that it resembled "one's first experience of Joyce and Lawrence . . . and it may turn out to be even more significant." In what follows I shall be concerned only with his books, dealing in this chapter with his criticism and writings on politics and social life, which cannot easily be separated from each other.

His first book, *We Moderns*, was published in 1919

under the name of "Edward Moore," and is a collection
of aphorisms from his contributions to *The New Age*. He
wished it to be forgotten. It was written, he himself said,
in "a sort of pinchbeck Nietzschean prose peppered with
exclamation marks,"[1] and expressed some attitudes
which he was to outgrow. In it he is immature, confused,
unused to dealing with ideas; he self-consciously advances paradoxical and challenging statements in order
to shock; some of the attitudes expressed are second-
hand, and not really in accordance with his deeper experience. Yet there is something moving about the book
all the same—in the young clerk's aspirations after heroic
virtue and fullness of life. There is wisdom and originality
in the book too, and some of the aphorisms are expressed
with brilliant and witty concision. The central theme is
an attack upon realism in modern art—especially in the
novel and in drama. It is not, he says, the business of the
artist to copy the surface of life, but to go deeper, to
reveal meaning, to convey an imaginative vision. "The
aim of Art was once to enrich existence by the creation
of gods and demi-gods; it is now to duplicate existence
by the portrayal of man. Art has become Imitation. . . ."[2]
Modern artists deal with sordid and trivial themes, and
do not even attempt the higher kinds such as tragedy.
This is seen especially in the treatment of love. Sex used
to be treated within the bounds of a well-understood
convention, from which the physiological was strictly
excluded; but the moderns have become impatient of
what they think artificial, "as if Art could be anything
but artificial!"[3] A similar debasement is found in life as
in art. "The ceremonious in manners arose from the
recognition that between the sexes there must be distance
—respect as well as intimacy—understanding. . . . But
now distance and understanding have alike disap-
peared."[4] This decadence he connects with materialism
and with industrialism. Artists have succumbed to the
environment, have lost their sense of power and their

sense of the possible greatness of man. "The worst evil of
our time is this, that there is nothing greater than the
current average existence to which man can look. . . .[5]
It is for the artist to take the lead in reversing this trend.
"Against this aimless Realism, we must oppose idealiza-
tion, especially that which is its highest expression,
Myth."[6] This condemnation of realism is not a call to
escape from life into an ivory tower, but to look deeper
into life. Mere aesthetes are condemned equally with the
realists; for, while true creators "write of certain
realities behind life," the aesthetes write only "of the
words standing for those realities."[7] Nor did he wish to
escape from the spiritual poverty he found in modern
life through "reactionary backdoors," among which he
at that time included Christianity. He tried to formulate
a positive, forward-looking faith. There are no absolute,
static values. "Eternal Love, or God is . . . eternal
creation, eternal change, eternal Becoming. Con-
sequently there is no absolute goal, no Perfection, except that which is realized at every moment in the
self-expression of Love."[8]

There is much in *We Moderns* that Muir grew out of—
the cult of the Superman, the condemnation of sympathy
("creative Love would enjoin, not sympathy with suffering, but the will to transcend suffering"),[9] of humility
and equality ("the great fosterers of the mediocre"),[10]
and of penitence; these things were taken second-hand
from Nietzsche. *We Moderns* lacks the balance and sanity
of his later works; but it is an interesting and at times, in
its ardour, moving book, and contains insights which he
had no need later to repudiate. The deadening, de-
personalising effect of a life of routine in modern industrial societies; the need to make possible a fuller,
freer life for the spirit, the imagination, the senses; the
contribution which art ought to make towards the libera-
tion of man from his immediate environment—these
were to remain among his central themes.

His next prose book, *Latitudes* (1924), is a collection of essays in literary criticism. More than half of them were written several years before publication, and were a sort of argument with himself which he had to undertake before starting the work of criticism. By 1924 he already disagreed with some of the opinions expressed in them, which are similar to those we found in *We Moderns*. The main stress is on the rejection of static, absolute values, on the assertion of life, of Becoming. Man is constantly tempted to check the free flow of the creative spirit by constructing fixed absolutes—in religion, in philosophy and in morals. Life is eternal Becoming, newness, uniqueness, change. Art has a large part to play in releasing man from his self-imposed bonds. Art is (in no trivial sense) play. Art "does not moralize or humanize us, nor remind us of eternal justice; it carries us into a world which is neither necessary nor necessitated, but perfectly arbitrary and free; and gives us freely something inconceivably rich and magical."[11] These attitudes were natural in one who was seeking to escape from the frustrations of his Glasgow existence into a fuller life. His childhood intuition of an order, a harmony of a non-constricting kind had been lost. In so far as industrial life, as he had known it, was an order, it was one which cramped the human spirit. The rather superficial Christianity of his earlier days also seemed to him to have been constricting. He was a refugee from Scottish puritanism. Later he was to be able to harmonise his conceptions of order and freedom; but he was to remain to the end hostile of the idea of fixed, static absolutes. Mrs Muir records that at the very end of his life, when waiting to be taken off to hospital, he said to her with great urgency: "There are no absolutes, no absolutes."[12]

The first nine essays in *Latitudes*, written later, are more mature. They are mostly studies of particular authors, and show him already able to write with

c

authority on Dostoyevsky, Nietzsche, Ibsen, Stendhal, as well as on Scottish writers. His knowledge of English literature at this time was patchy. His criticism is always original, sometimes penetrating, though not always well-balanced. He writes well of Burns and of the Scottish ballads; but is still prone to exaggeration—as in his treatment of "George Douglas" (George Douglas Brown) and in his slighting references to Stevenson—and to hasty generalisation. His writing has wit and freshness, and conveys a sense of urgency, a feeling that the books he deals with really matter to him. Criticism, he says, should not be absolutely distinguished from creative writing. "The subject-matter of all artists is life," and the critic is (or should be) a special kind of artist who "chooses for treatment that expression of life which is art." To the critic of this kind a book is "the starting point for an enquiry into the human spirit."[13] Muir's own best criticism has zest and urgency because it is an attempt to explore the deepest levels of experience, not just to evaluate books.

Transition (1926) is a series of essays on contemporary writers and on the situation of the creative artist in an age of transition. In past ages when certain orders of values were accepted, writers, whether or not they themselves accepted these values, were helped by living in an intelligible world to give their work completeness. In this age of transition there has been a gain in complexity, but a loss in wholeness. In fiction characters and emotions tend to be so minutely analysed that we are left with a mass of fragments rather than whole human beings. Writers' uncertainties give their work "an air either of vacillation or of violence."[14] Muir is not here writing nostalgically about an idealised past. He is concerned more with the achievements of contemporary writers than with their limitations, with the new possibilities that were being opened up than with the difficulties. A problem which he does not give any clear answer to is whether criticism itself must be in a state of flux in an age of transition, or whether there are permanent standards which can always be applied. He divides writers into three classes—the fashionable (*e.g.*, Aldous Huxley) who merely reflect the *zeitgeist*, those who try to escape from it (*e.g.*, D. H. Lawrence), and those who struggle against it (*e.g.*, Joyce). It is the last two classes, especially the last, who are the real creators. "It is he who wrestles with the age who finally justifies both it and himself."[15] This seems to imply the existence of some permanent standards, since there can be no virtue in wrestling with one's age except if it be in the name of some values higher than the merely fashionable ones; but this line of argument is not followed up.

All this is fairly commonplace, and it is not the chapters, the first and the last two, in which these ideas are discussed that give lasting value to the book, but rather the middle ones in which particular writers (Joyce, Lawrence, Virginia Woolf, Stephen Hudson, Aldous Huxley, Strachey, Eliot, Edith Sitwell, Graves) are studied. Fortunately these writers are considered not only in terms of their relation to the *zeitgeist*. The criticism is always original and often illuminating. It surprises one at first, for instance, to read that "as a poet Mr. Eliot lacks seriousness";[16] but the essay on Eliot contains in a few pages more suggestive observations than many subsequent long studies. The stridency of some of Muir's earlier writings has been left behind, and the criticism is better balanced than before. Though he had only a small proportion of the works of some of his authors to judge by, his assessments are still worth reading.

His next critical book, his first written as a whole, was *The Structure of the Novel* (1928). It is beautifully-written —in a quiet, yet vigorous, and perfectly lucid prose. By this time he had himself begun to write novels; this and the interest in the subject aroused by E. M. Forster's *Aspects of the Novel* and Percy Lubbock's *The Craft of*

Fiction led him to make his own investigation into the principles of structure in the novel. It is a particularly difficult subject. Novels are so varied that they resist classification; one can hardly say anything about "the novel" in general without thinking of exceptions. Muir's classification of novels under three main headings enables him to make many illuminating comments on particular works, but is not, I think, any more universally valid than other such attempts have been. One can classify novels in many different ways, all of which may be useful for some purposes, but none of which is final, or adequate to the complexity of the subject.

One of the most interesting themes discussed is the treatment of time in different novels. In what he calls the "dramatic" novel (*e.g., Wuthering Heights*) "time is incarnated and articulated in the characters; its speed therefore is psychological, determined by the slowness or rapidity of the action."[17] There is a sense of inevitability, of fate, of the action necessarily moving towards a predestined end. At the end "the particular action will have completed itself, bringing about an equilibrium, or issuing in some catastrophe which cannot be pursued farther."[18] In the "chronicle" novel (*e.g., War and Peace*), on the other hand, there is still a sense of fate, of inevitability, but of a different kind. In *War and Peace* the speed of time

is not determined by the intensity of the action; it has, on the contrary, a cold and deadly regularity, which is external to the characters and unaffected by them. The characters grow, or grow old. The emphasis is on that. . . . Change . . . is not organic with the action, now rapid, now almost stationary, coinciding with the movements of the passions and the feelings; it follows the remote astronomical course which for mankind determines time's measurement; it is regular, arithmetical, and in a sense inhuman and featureless.[19]

Within this rigid framework of time we see life in all its variety of accidents. The difference between the two kinds of novels can be seen in the manner in which the chief characters die:

Captain Ahab, Michael Henchard, Catherine Earnshaw make their exits at the moment which fate has long prepared for them. But Prince Andrew is snuffed out accidentally, at the time when he is planning and resolving how to live.[20]

At the end of *War and Peace* there is a sense of time going on, whereas at the end of *Wuthering Heights* and of *Moby Dick* there is a sense of finality.

Quotation and summary can give but a faint idea of the number and subtlety of Muir's observations on the handling of space and time in different novels. This book is a concentrated one, and demands to be read as a whole and with care. It is his one critical book in which he was able to develop a sustained argument at length, and makes one wish that he had had leisure to do so more often. It is of interest for the light it throws not only on the novels considered in it but on Muir's own other works. In his criticism, as in his poetry, he was grappling with fundamental problems. In *The Structure of the Novel* he was trying not only to see how different novels are constructed, but to define the different ways in which in life we apprehend space and time and perceive meaning in our experience.

During the nineteen-twenties Muir lived abroad and in the country in England, and devoted his energies to his work as poet, critic, and translator; but his letters to his sister and brother-in-law in Glasgow showed his continued interest in Scottish affairs and in politics. By 1927 he knew C. M. Grieve, whom he greatly admired. He wrote to his sister, Mrs Thorburn:

Grieve is a strong nationalist, republican, socialist, and everything that is out and out. He thinks that if Scotland were a nation we would have Scottish literature, art, music, culture, everything that other nations seem to have and we haven't. I think that would probably be likely; but I feel rather detached, as I've often told Grieve because after all I'm not Scotch, I'm an Orkneyman.

This "I'm not Scotch" goes too far, and he partially repudiates it: "But this is nonsense, I'm afraid, though there's some sense in it." He would have liked to have had the sense of belonging to a united Scottish nation. Such a nation had existed, he thought, in the distant past ("Long since we were a family, a people"),[21] and might exist again in the future; but he found present-day Scotland a difficult place for a poet to find a home and an accepted position in.

The cultural poverty, compared to what might have been, of modern Scotland is explained by history; so Muir was dealing with matters of immediate concern to him when a commission to write a life of John Knox made him turn in 1928 to a study of Scottish history in the sixteenth century. The biography, he later admitted, was "too full of dislike for Knox and certain things in Scottish life."[22] Its virtues and vices are connected, the author's lively concern with his subject making it more fresh and, at times, penetrating than most academic histories, but at the same time distorting the perspective. I believe he much exaggerates the influence of one man in concluding: "What Knox really did was to rob Scotland of all the benefits of the Renaissance."[23] Further, he probably gives insufficient prominence to the good things which Knox did and tried to do—for instance, for education. Knox failed to achieve all he wanted, but he and the other Reformers should be given some credit for the relatively high standard of Scottish education in the succeeding centuries as well as blamed for the things in Scottish life (for instance the "universal and reciprocal

fault-finding" encouraged by the Presbyterian system of
Church discipline), which Muir and other recent writers
have justifiably disliked. Muir's portrait of Knox as a
sadistic religious fanatic is supported by a good deal of
evidence from his writings, but I imagine it is rather a
one-sided one.

A few years later he turned to present-day Scotland,
which had been hit, even worse than England, by the
economic depression of the early nineteen-thirties.
Driving one summer evening through the ugly mining
districts of Lanarkshire and seeing at street corners
groups of idle, sullen-looking young men, whose lives
had been deprived of all purpose and meaning by lack
of work, he decided to write a book about modern Scotland. He was given an old car, toured the country, and
recorded his impressions in *Scottish Journey* (1935). Starting from Edinburgh, he went south to Jedburgh, then
west through the Border Country and north to Glasgow;
then across to Angus and up through the Highlands and
to the Orkneys. The book contains some sensitive descriptions of weather and of scenery, but is much more than a
conventional travelogue or tourist's guide. He was concerned not with the picturesque nor the historic, but
with the lives of the ordinary people of Scotland. He
paints rather a gloomy picture. In the towns, though the
poverty was not so extreme as it had been in his youth,
industrialism had largely eliminated the graces of life,
and now, by its failure, had deprived many thousands
even of work to give meaning to their lives in ugly surroundings. In the country, agriculture was not in a prosperous state; the farm workers were poor, and dependent
for their livelihood on the whims of the farmers. In the
Highlands, he found still a dignified and courteous
people; but the area had been depopulated and its
ancient culture to a large extent destroyed as a result of
a series of calamities—the severities that followed Cul-
loden, the Clearances, the rise of tourism and the turning

of a large part of the land into a huge game preserve. Only
among the small and prosperous farms in Orkney did he
find an alive and contented community.

As a remedy for these evils he did not imagine that it
was possible to take the life of the small farmers of
Orkney as a model. Industrialism had to be accepted,
and transformed, humanized. He was a Nationalist, but
with reservations. He did not think that the mere restitu-
tion of a Scottish Parliament would cure the ills of the
country. He regretted that the Nationalists, in order to
attract people of every shade of political opinion, had
deprived themselves of the possibility of making any
definite statement of economic policy. Only, he thought,
by an economic policy along socialist or Douglasite lines
would a new, prosperous, and united Scotland be
brought into being.

This summary may have given the impression of a
gloomy, perhaps cranky, book; but it is one of great
interest and, at times, of great beauty. It contains sharp
and humorous portraits of people encountered and of
incidents on the way. (The humour of some of the incidents is increased for those who remember the author's
incompetence with machines and absent-mindedness as
a driver.) The descriptions have a poetic quality.
Throughout there is a deep compassionate concern for
people. Most of what he has to say is by no means out of
date.

Muir followed up his discussion in *Scottish Journey* of
means to create a new Scotland by a pamphlet, *Social
Credit and the Labour Party* (1935), addressed to a friend
whom he had worked with in the I.L.P. in his Glasgow
days. He argued that the best way to advance towards
Socialism was by putting into practice the ideas on social
credit of Major C. H. Douglas. The object of socialist
parties is to take over for the community the means of
production, distribution, and exchange. The three are
connected, but there is no reason why one should not

start with one of them. The Labour Party gives most
attention to the taking over of the means of production,
whereas the Douglasites would begin by taking over the
means of exchange, by nationalising credit. I am not
competent to judge the economic soundness of Major
Douglas' theories. I suspect that Muir was not either.
He was drawn into enthusiasm for them by his association with Orage. Social Credit was attractive to those
who, like Muir, wished for a new society, but were
repelled by Communism; for it seemed to them the most
hopeful means of achieving the transition peacefully.

In his next book, *Scott and Scotland* (1936), Muir turned
his attention to that aspect of Scottish life which most
nearly concerned the writer, language. For three hundred years or more Scottish literature has been stunted
by the lack of a national language capable of unifying
the country and expressing its whole mind. The educated
have turned more and more to standard English, in
which most serious literature has been written. Scots has
been used, until recently, only for simple poetry on rather
a narrow range of subjects and for short stories. It has
expressed only a fragment of the national mind. Scots-
men have achieved distinction as writers of English—
especially in expository prose, such as history, philosophy,
treatises on economics, etc.; but have been at a disadvantage when attempting imaginative literature in a
language which is, to some extent at least, alien to them.

> Scotsmen feel in one language and think in another. ...
> Scots poetry can only be revived ... when Scotsmen
> begin to think *naturally* in Scots. The curse of Scottish
> literature is the lack of a whole language, which
> finally means the lack of a whole mind.[24]

Most Scottish writers would in general agree with this
diagnosis. Muir was more controversial, however, when
he came to say what should be done. Other Scottish
writers in his time were trying, by taking words from

different dialects and periods and by inventing new ones,
to create an educated Scots suitable for all purposes.
Muir was sceptical of the possibility of doing this. He
thought that the Scottish writer must accept English as
his medium:

> The practical present-day problem may be put some-
> what as follows: that a Scottish writer who wishes to
> achieve some approximation to completeness has no
> choice except to absorb the English tradition, and that
> if he thoroughly does so his work belongs not merely to
> Scottish literature but to English literature as well. On
> the other hand, if he wishes to add to an indigenous
> Scottish literature, and roots himself deliberately in
> Scotland, he will find there, no matter how long he
> may search, neither an organic community to round
> off his conceptions, nor a major literary tradition to
> support him, nor even a faith among the people them-
> selves that a Scottish literature is possible or desirable,
> nor any opportunity, finally, of making a livelihood
> by his work.[25]

So his conclusion is that "Scotland can only create a
national literature by writing in English."[26]

This is not the place to pursue this still controversial
subject. There seems to be an inadequately filled hiatus
between Muir's diagnosis and his prescription. His own
work, however, both in verse and prose (and, more
recently, that of Norman MacCaig) is a sufficient
demonstration that it is possible for a Scottish writer to
express himself in English. At the same time one may
conjecture that the rather late flowering of his poetry
was partly due to difficulty with his medium. Also it is
possible that he might have been able to put more colour
into his work if he had been able to use the same language
as he had heard spoken round him in youth. His situation,
of course, was rather different from that of other Scottish
writers in that he was an Orcadian and never, perhaps,

felt altogether at home in Southern Scotland. For him to have adopted Lowland Scots as his medium would have been to use a language almost as alien to him as standard English. His solution may well have been right for him without necessarily being so for others.

Muir's last work on Scotland, a pamphlet *The Scots and their Country*, written for the British Council in 1946, contains an appreciative and well-balanced analysis of the Scottish character as formed by history.

During and after these excursions into Scottish affairs, and into politics, the incessant business of making a living as a translator and writer for periodicals went on. Immediate needs and his more important work as a poet did not allow him leisure to plan and carry out any major critical works in his own way and in his own time. The only books of criticism produced in his later life were a commissioned work, *The Present Age* (1939), written for the series *Introductions to English Literature*, and a miscellaneous collection of essays, *Essays on Literature and Society* (1946). *The Present Age* seems to have been written rather hastily. The bibliography is inadequate and unreliable; and, though it contains an interesting analysis of some of the social and other changes that affected literature, the book is not altogether satisfactory as a comprehensive survey of the period. These defects, however, are more than made up for by the originality and acuteness of the criticisms of particular books and authors. *Essays on Literature and Society* covers a wide field—German, Scottish and English writers as well as some general problems. Muir was one of the least "provincial" of critics.

It is not possible to sum up his critical standpoint in any neat formula. It may seem distressingly vague to say that he was a "humane" critic. By this I mean that he judged works as wholes, a writer's work as a whole and literature by more than narrowly aesthetic standards. Further his criticism conveys a sense of enjoyment, of

zest and adventure. Literary criticism has recently tended
to become more professional and specialised. Lines and
passages have been analysed with great care; and special
aspects of writers' works—syntax, diction, patterns of
imagery, etc.—have been examined minutely. There has
been a gain in precision, but sometimes a loss of ability to
give a just description of the total effect a work makes,
and to relate literature to life. Muir was unaffected by
fashion, and belongs to the central, humane and liberal
tradition of criticism. He was capable of detailed analysis,
as in his essay on Hölderlin's *Patmos*, but did not often
go in for explication of texts. He was concerned with the
imaginative truth of what a writer conveys, and with
details of style only in so far as these are a writer's means
of embodying his vision. As we have seen, he thought
that criticism could be the starting point for "an inquiry
into the human spirit." In his criticism he was seeking
the help of other writers to probe into the heights and
depths of human experience, and into the big problems
he was concerned with in his other works—time, the
nature of the good society, etc. This means that for him
literary criticism could not be a self-contained thing. It
does not mean, however, that he was interested in a
writer's opinions rather than his works, nor that his standards of judgment were narrowly moralistic. He was able
to appreciate such writers as Hardy and D. H. Lawrence,
with whose opinions he did not agree, and was well
aware that it is the imaginative truth of the total vision
that a writer's work conveys that matters rather than his
opinions.

An example of how he relates literature to larger issues
can be seen in his essay on "The Decline of the Novel."[27]
He starts by considering the endings of some older and
some modern novels. In the traditional novel the ending
may be banal or it may be tragic, but in either case there
is a sense of completeness, of a story having been told. In
the characteristic modern novel, on the other hand, "the

ending is really a sort of beginning, the beginning of a quite different story. . . . Such endings are expressions of hope of completion, arrows shot into the irresponsive future." Examples are the endings of *Sons and Lovers* and of *Portrait of the Artist as a Young Man*. At one time he might have commended such endings as according with his idea of eternal becoming; but now he lays more stress on the need for wholeness, for completeness in a work of art. "A story without an ending describes a mode of existence which has not been thought out and stops short of meaning." For events to be seen to have meaning, for a story to be able to be completed, it is necessary to be able to see human life within some wider framework. The lack of such a framework is the reason for the fragmentariness of much modern art:

> The conception of life which prevails today is a conception of life purely in time. The contemporary novel is a story of time against a background of time. The traditional novel is a story of time against a permanent pattern. . . . Seen against eternity the life of man is a complete story. Seen against time it is an unfinished one, a part of endless change, a fleeting picture on an unstable substance.[28]

One's outstanding impression of his later criticism is of its scrupulous integrity and fairness. He was quite free from personal and political bias, and even from the more justifiable bias of the practitioner in favour of writers whose works have helped him or against those whose influence he has had to escape from. We have seen his dislike in early days of the "realist" or "period" novel. If his mature criticism has any bias, it is, perhaps, still against any writer who seemed to him to do no more than describe the surface of life and to reflect contemporary attitudes. His demand that a writer should not just describe, but reveal meaning, offer a fresh vision, is a perfectly proper one; but it may lead to the under-

rating of writers who express an imaginative vision
through solid, realistic description. In common with
many other moderns, he was, perhaps, unwilling to give
enough credit for the ability to tell a good and entertaining story, or simply to be funny. He was more at home
with the profound and the tragic than with the honestly
superficial or the comic. But even when dealing with
writers whom he did not greatly admire he tried to see
and to state fairly anything that could be said in their
favour.

His critical writing, though consistently serious, is
saved from solemnity or dullness by its zest and its wit.
It is full of brilliantly epigrammatic phrases, though he
was not in his mature work led, as nearly all epigram-
matists are, by the desire to be striking into saying something other than what he really means. His wit is not a
mere surface brilliance. One could pick out dozens of
quotable sentences from *The Present Age*, for instance:

Of Shaw:

His prose is direct, concise, vigorous: an admirable
instrument for putting the case *against* anything.[29]

Of T. F. Powys:

Mr. Powys gives the impression that he knows a disreputable secret about life, but does not convince us
that the real secret of life is disreputable.[30]

Of Virginia Woolf:

She writes about the ordinary passions of men and
women as if she had been told about them by some one
who regarded them as interesting but unreasonable
and therefore, like Pound's Hell, "for other people".[31]

The wit here is being used to convey insight concisely and
strikingly. The plan of *The Present Age* meant that he had
to give brief assessments of many authors without being
able to devote much space to any. Within the limits im-
posed he managed to pack in an extraordinary amount
of incisive comment.

Muir did much to keep alive traditions of humane values and of literary standards in a time of uncertainty on the one hand and of narrow dogmatism on the other, and to counteract the provincialism of much English criticism. In *The Structure of the Novel* and elsewhere he threw out many suggestive general ideas about literature and about the relation of literature to larger matters. In *Transition*, in *The Present Age*, in his introductions to the translations of Kafka, etc., he gave incisive and well-balanced assessments of particular writers, which are still, and will remain, worth reading. But he did not make any important contributions to the theory of literary criticism. The conditions in which he worked did not allow him to achieve the major critical works that he might otherwise have written. It is, surely, as a poet, not as a critic, that he will live.

REFERENCES

1. *A.*, p. 127.
2. *W.M.*, p. 159.
3. *W.M.*, p. 27.
4. *W.M.*, p. 20.
5. *W.M.*, p. 172.
6. *W.M.*, p. 173.
7. *W.M.*, pp. 51–2.
8. *W.M.*, p. 184.
9. *W.M.*, pp. 180–1.
10. *W.M.*, p. 153.
11. *L.*, p. 141.
12. *Encounter*, Dec. 1960, p. 52.
13. *L.*, p. 141.
14. *T.*, p. 204.
15. *T.*, p. 7.
16. *T.*, p. 141.
17. *S.N.*, p. 98.
18. *S.N.*, p. 58.
19. *S.N.*, pp. 98–9.
20. *S.N.*, p. 109.
21. "The Ring," in *C.P.*, p. 113.
22. *A.*, p. 231.
23. *K.*, p. 309.
24. *S.S.*, pp. 21–2.
25. *S.S.*, pp. 14–15.
26. *S.S.*, p. 178.
27. *L.S.*, pp. 144–50.
28. *L.S.*, pp. 148–9.
29. *P.A.*, p. 160.
30. *P.A.*, p. 151.
31. *P.A.*, p. 139.

CHAPTER III

THE NOVELIST AND AUTOBIOGRAPHER

Fairly early in his career as a writer Muir wrote three novels—*The Marionette* (1927), *The Three Brothers* (1931), and *Poor Tom* (1932). I wish I had read them before reading the *Autobiography*. It would then have been easier to have appreciated them for what they are in themselves. Coming from the *Autobiography* one cannot help noticing the presence in them of incidents and situations adapted from the life, and so, perhaps, one fails to judge them fairly as independent works. Nevertheless I am confident that Muir's talent was for reflective writing rather than for narrative or the creation of character. The dialogue is, for the most part, unconvincing and lacking in vitality. The characters are mostly either spokesmen for the author or have but a shadowy existence. None of the women come alive. The novels are convincing only, or almost only, when Muir is dealing with the inner lives of characters in some ways resembling himself, when he is working out through them his own problems and conflicts, and when he is describing, under a thin disguise, events which had moved him in actual life.

The Marionette, unusually for a first novel, is the one which stands up best on its own without reference to Muir's life. This is, perhaps, because there is no character in it who is too close to being a reflection of himself. Though, of course, using his own experience, he had to make an effort of imagination to create the central character, a feeble-minded Austrian boy living with his father near Salzburg. This motherless boy is unable to grow up. He is isolated from people, and is afraid of animals: "He saw nature as a terrifying heraldry. The cat, the lizard, and the wasp were embattled forces armed for war, carrying terror and death in their blazoned stripes, their stings, claws, and tongues."[1] After his fourteenth birthday his father begins to take an interest in him, and gives him dolls and a doll's house, out of which he makes a fantasy world. He takes him for walks, one day for a long walk through Salzburg and up a mountain. The boy's impressions on this day are vividly described; he is frightened by the bustle of the Salzburg streets, by the falling of a fir-cone, by the smallness of things seen from the top of the mountain, by a dog, and by salamanders. This is one of the most impressive parts of the book, and reproduces in heightened form, as Muir admitted,[2] the author's own impressions of Salzburg as a newcomer in 1923. Here the actual experiences are successfully transmuted into fiction. The evocation of the boy's nightmare world is a real act of imaginative creation. Later his father takes the boy to several performances in a marionette theatre; this enables him to create a richer fantasy world in which he imagines himself taking part—he is Faust, and in love with Gretchen. The successive inner worlds of imagination in which he finds satisfaction are threatened by incursions from the outer world—by an accident at the theatre in which the Gretchen puppet is damaged and is seen to be but a doll, by boys looking over the wall at him and shouting "loony." He comes to believe that his Gretchen is dead, but in the end finds peace in a dream in which he revives her. An early reviewer[3] asked "why the emotions and reactions of a half-witted boy should have any but a pathological importance." He felt that some symbolical meanings must be present behind the incidents, but that the author had failed to make them sufficiently clear. It is not necessary to look for any precise symbolical meanings. It is sufficient that the boy's reactions, his dreams and fantasies, are made vivid to the imagination. Muir gives to the boy some of his own

D

dreams, which he recorded later in the *Autobiography* and used in his poems. He was, perhaps, trying to understand them by objectifying them, and was displaying in the boy a more extreme case than his own of the difficulty of reconciling the inner and the outer worlds, the dreaming and the waking self. It is interesting to compare the different appearances in his work of recurrent dream *motifs*. But *The Marionette* is worth reading, not only in relation to his other work, but also for the poetic quality which it has in itself.

The Three Brothers Muir referred to in letters to his sister as "my novel on Scottish life in the 16th century" and as "the best thing I've done up till now." In it he used the reading he had recently been doing for his life of Knox. The story is set in St Andrews and Edinburgh in the twenty years or so after the murder of Cardinal Beaton in 1546. We hear of the murder, see something of the civil war, catch a glimpse of Mary, Queen of Scots, in procession up Edinburgh High Street, and hear much discussion of the religious controversies of the time. But as an historical novel *The Three Brothers* is not satisfying. We do not really feel ourselves to be in the sixteenth century. The discussions on religion contain interesting ideas, but are not dramatically convincing as the speech of real people. Muir is able to reflect intelligently about the Scottish past, but not to recreate it. Beneath the historical theme is the private one of the relationship of the Blackadder brothers—and with this Muir's emotions were more deeply involved. He had felt acutely the early, painful and wasteful deaths of his own brothers, Willie and Johnnie, with whom his relationship had been close but not without strife. After they were gone nothing could be done in life to put right anything that had been wrong between them. Hence the need to resurrect the past, to transform it by imagination into a work of art and so to release himself from it. This may have been the psychological reason, perhaps unconscious, which led

Muir to treat in *The Three Brothers* and in *Poor Tom* of the relationship of brothers, and to describe in the first a death similar in some ways to that of Willie and in the second one even more like that of Johnnie. This does not mean, of course, that the Blackadder brothers in *The Three Brothers* or the Mansons in *Poor Tom* are to be identified with the Muirs, or that any of the incidents in the novels can be assumed to have had counterparts in real life, except when we know from the *Autobiography* that they did. In connection with *Poor Tom* Muir warned his sister not to "look for any living model (or dead one either) for any of the characters: that would be completely wrong, for they are all synthetic, made up of scraps taken from all sorts of nooks and corners, and mostly pure imagination, like the main situation." He was trying to write fiction, not autobiography; and, if he had written successfully—if, that is, the incidents and characters were consistently convincing in their places in the novels—then we would not be tempted to mention his life at all. But, unfortunately, the effect the novels make is patchy; some parts seem much more real than others; the different elements do not cohere to make a consistent whole. As the stories get under way, the rather fragile construction made by Muir the novelist is increasingly overwhelmed by the weight of the actual past, with which Muir the man was trying to come to terms. The incursions of the actual past into the novels is destructive to them as works of art because the reality of some parts reveals the flimsiness of others. Parts are produced by the not very powerful imagination of a novelist trying to tell stories about fictional characters, parts by the powerful imagination of a poet brooding over his own experience. Though the novels are not wholly satisfactory as fiction, the presence of the poet in them results in their containing moving and memorable passages, which make them more worth reading than many more nearly perfect works.

In *The Three Brothers* Muir tried to distance the material from his own life by creating an historical setting; but the impressive parts of the book are not those which deal with the outer world of events, with action and the ordinary surface of life, but those which reveal the inner world of David Blackadder's thoughts and emotions and imaginings—his bewilderment when first encountering the life of a great city, his loss of religious faith and his efforts to regain it, his dreams (especially these). In *Poor Tom* there is less attempt than in the other two to distance the material from real life. The setting is Glasgow in, one supposes, the early twentieth century. The Manson family have come from a northern island; the father has died of a heart attack. Tom Manson is adventurous, had wanted to go to sea, is ill at ease in Glasgow; he falls off a tram-car when drunk, gets a tumour on the brain, and dies after great agony (like Johnnie Muir). Mansie Manson, his brother, is more sensitive and intelligent, has intellectual friends; is converted to religion, and then to socialism; joins the Clarion Scouts, and has a sense of exhilaration during a May Day parade; is greatly affected by his brother's illness and death. The "main situation," which Muir says, no doubt truly, is from imagination, is presumably the three-cornered relationship between the two brothers and a girl, Helen Williamson. This strand in the story is not at all effectively realised. The things in the novel which strike one as real are, in general, those which are closest to things found in the *Autobiography*—Tom's illness and death, Mansie's intellectual and moral struggles. Mansie is certainly not intended as a self-portrait. At the beginning trouble is taken to differentiate him from Muir himself—he is made rather priggish, dandified, successful at business, older than Tom (Muir was only seventeen when his considerably older brother, Johnnie, died); but, as the story warms up, the mask slips, Mansie becomes more likable, more alive—with his creator's life rather than a fictional life of his own. Despite its imperfections, *Poor Tom* is a moving and interesting book. The setting and the incidents are more vividly presented than in *The Three Brothers*. The ferment of ideas in the young Mansie's mind—about time, religion, socialism, etc., as well as in connection with his brother's death—is, at times, movingly brought home to us.

Our conclusion must be that Muir had not enough of the particular kind of imagination that a novelist requires to achieve success in this form. Nevertheless, these novels bring one into contact with a fine mind confronting deeply-felt experience and thinking with originality about the ultimate issues of life. A poet's imagination is at work in them.

As we have seen, in his successive novels Muir approached more closely towards a direct treatment of his own past. This may have led him to decide that the proper way to deal with the material was in an undisguised autobiography. However that may be, at St Andrews he wrote *The Story and the Fable* (1940). This tells the story of his life up to the time when, at Dresden at the age of thirty-five, he recovered from the long illness which had seized him when he had gone to Glasgow, up to the time when he began to write poetry. The best part is that on his childhood. The early chapters are one of the most beautiful accounts of a childhood ever written. The simple, uninflated, yet quietly rhythmical prose convinces one of the authenticity of the experiences described. The part on Glasgow is also impressive, but strikes one as giving only a partial account of his life and of himself. No doubt he tells us all that seemed to him most important. He concentrates mainly on his inner life, though he is capable of presenting vivid pictures of things seen. He may give some the impression of an excessively gloomy and even self-absorbed young man. His account needs to be supplemented by the memories of others who stress his gaiety and charm as a companion, his passionate involvement in Guild Socialism, etc.

The book is not mainly a record of events. Beneath the story he tries to see the fable, to understand his own life and to see it in relation to other lives and to the life of the race. It is an essay in self-knowledge—and much more than that. It is an enquiry into the ultimate meaning of human life, and of society. It records a search to recover lost innocence, to find again the right road from which he had wandered. It is comparable, in some ways, to Traherne's *Centuries of Meditation*. Muir is very humble, and very honest. Though the book by its nature is centred on himself, he is not concerned with himself alone. He had experienced the deadening effect of a life of routine in an industrial society, and had escaped into the comparative leisure and freedom of his years of wandering abroad; but he was very conscious that others had not, and could not:

> Life to the vast majority of people now is merely the machinery of life. The only justification for society is that it should make possible a life of the imagination and the spirit, a life at least of the senses, since even that is infinitely above a life of routine, which is a sort of no-life. But society has not yet solved its most elementary problems, and I do not think it will find it easy to solve them.[4]

This last sentence is rather a banal conclusion, and in this book he offers no direct help to the solution of the problems of society—though elsewhere, as we have seen, he did. But even here, by looking beneath the surface of his own life, he was trying to diagnose not only his own sickness, and to find the road out of the labyrinth not only for himself. But he does not preach, nor claim to have found any easy solutions. At the end he claims no more than that he has attained to a certain amount of self-knowledge and to a realisation that at least there is a road towards a freer and fuller life:

> I leave my fragmentary record at this point, the point at which, by imaginatively understanding my own life as a human being, I began to understand human life not as a life of routine and machinery, but as a fable extending far beyond the experience given to us by our senses and our practical reason. My road to that realization is not, I feel, a typical one; perhaps, indeed, it was fantastically abnormal; but there must be countless roads to it, and this was mine. The realization itself was merely a beginning, and did not carry me more than one step on the road I should go. Indeed, it did very little more than tell me that the road is there, and that it is determined by my beginning and my end and my relations with other creatures and with the spirit which moves through all creatures. But to deal with that another book would be required, a more severe and exact one, and perhaps one which I am incapable of writing. So for the present I leave it.[5]

So he breaks off, adding only some very interesting extracts from a diary 1937–9 to cover the later years.

Thirteen years later he took up the story of his life again, and added seven new chapters in place of the extracts from the diary to bring the story up to his time at Newbattle. If we expect this later part of the *Autobiography* (1954) to be the "more severe and exact book" tracing the stages of his progress along his road, we may be disappointed. There is more of story than of fable in it, though there are memorable passages that belong to the fable—his realisation of his Christianity at St Andrews and of the splendours of Christendom in Rome. By this time his deeper self was going into his poetry, and it is there that we must follow his journey back to the recovery of the lost Eden. The later part of the *Autobiography* is more scrappy, has less intensity and unity, than the part written earlier. We are glad to have the new chapters, but it is *The Story and the Fable* which is the great book. Nevertheless these new chapters are of great interest. He comments shrewdly, and always with sympathy, on people and events—on friends, on the "simple-lifers" met in South Germany after the first war, on the exponents of "free" love at St Tropez, on Communism and on the *coup d'état* in Prague. He writes a beautifully lucid, plain, but vigorous prose—not eccentric nor striving after effect, but always expressive of his individuality.

REFERENCES

1. *M.*, pp. 7–8.
2. *A.*, p. 215.
3. *Times Literary Supplement*, 19 May 1927.
4. *S.F.*, p. 236.
5. *Ibid.*

CHAPTER IV

THE POET: I

Even though some verses by "Edward Moore" had appeared earlier in *The New Age*, Muir rightly dated the beginning of his career as a poet from those leisured days in South Germany when he recovered from his inner conflicts, when his imagination woke, and his childhood came alive for him again. The start was difficult. "Though my imagination had begun to work I had no technique by which I could give expression to it. There were the rhythms of English poetry on the one hand, the images in my mind on the other. All I could do was to force the one, creaking and complaining, into the mould of the other."[1] Yet, he felt, there were some advantages in his situation in comparison with that of the young poet "who knows too much or thinks he knows too much about poetry, and can solve with ease the technical problems which I could not solve at all. To think of poetry like this makes it simple and business-like, and may make it almost a clever thing."[2] From the beginning his poetry had integrity; it was never facile. He was painfully trying to say something of his own, and in his own way.

Of the twenty-four poems in *First Poems* (1925) only nine are included in the final collected edition. Muir took a copy of *First Poems*, extensively revised some of the poems and wrote scathing comments on several of them. Even one of those which were retained, "Betrayal", he described as "very bad." The revisions are designed to exclude poetic diction ("o'er" is changed to "on," "viewless" to "hidden") and unnecessary adjectives, and to improve the terseness and precision of the writing ("changeless sky" is altered to "stone-smooth sky"). Anyone who wants to follow his development should read the whole volume and study the revisions, but I shall confine myself here to the nine retained poems. What strikes one immediately about these is that Muir is already speaking with an individual voice. One can, perhaps, detect the influence of Wordsworth; "Ballad of the Soul" can be compared, though hardly in quality, with Coleridge's "Ancient Mariner"; and the influence of the traditional Scottish ballads, such as Muir had heard his mother sing as a child, is certainly present. But none of these poems could have been written by anyone else.

The best of these early poems are the three which deal with childhood experiences which had come alive for him again. In "Childhood" he tries, with some success, to recreate his early sense of security, of timelessness and of unity with nature. He already shows here a Wordsworthian ability to make poetry out of simple, unemphatic words and straightforward prose constructions:

> Long time he lay upon the sunny hill,
>   To his father's house below securely bound. . . .
>
> Grey tiny rocks slept round him where he lay,
>   Moveless as they, more still as evening came,
> The grasses threw straight shadows far away,
>   And from the house his mother called his name.[3]

This poem merely returns into the past, and tries to recreate an experience without doing much with it. "Horses" attempts something more. It brings together the present and the past, the sight of horses ploughing in a bare field bringing back his childhood emotions with regard to the horses on his father's farm; and the feelings it contains are more complex, including fear and awe as well as rapture. There is some over-writing:

Their conquering hooves which trod the stubble down
Were ritual that turned the field to brown,
And their great hulks were seraphim of gold,
Or mute ecstatic monsters on the mould. . . .

Their eyes as brilliant and as wide as night
Gleamed with a cruel apocalyptic light. . . .[4]

One feels the presence of strong and genuine emotions
struggling for expression, but the words fail in precision.
Nevertheless the poem as a whole is impressive, and conveys a sense at once of kinship with animal life and of its
mysterious "otherness." These poems look back into the
past with nostalgia; "Ballad of Hector in Hades" deals
with a terrifying childhood experience, which he is now
able to face and release himself from. This poem, on
Achilles chasing Hector round the walls of Troy, is

> a resuscitation of the afternoon when I ran away, in
> real terror, from another boy as I returned from
> school. The bare landscape of the little island became,
> without my knowing it, a universal landscape over
> which Abraham and Moses and Achilles and Ulysses
> and Tristram and all sorts of pilgrims passed; and
> Troy was associated with the Castle, a mere green
> mound near my father's house.[5]

This is the best poem in the book. The use of myth has
enabled him to objectify his personal experiences, to
universalise it and make it into a work of art. It is not
necessary to know anything about Muir's life to appreciate it. It has something of the strength and vividness of a true ballad.

The poems arising out of more recent experiences are,
in general, less successful. Muir needed time for his
imagination to work upon the raw material given by
life. "Ballad of the Soul," originally called "Ballad of
Eternal Life," is of great interest, but perhaps more as a
psychological document than as a poem. It was excluded
from the collected edition of 1952, but restored in 1960,

having been extensively revised. Muir wrote above the original version: "This was a dream—at a time when I was being psycho-analysed. The dream was wonderful, and the poem is all wrong." The dream was recorded at the time, and discussed with his analyst.[6] Read on its own, the poem, even in its revised version, is bewildering. Compared with the prose version there does not seem to be much gain in vividness, nor any in intelligibility. It is not that one wishes the poet to explain the meanings of the successive visions, but he should convey more compellingly to the reader's imagination the feelings aroused by them. The trouble was partly lack of skill, and partly the fact that he was trying simply to reproduce what was given to him in the dream rather than letting his imagination work creatively on the given material to produce something new, a poem. "Ballad of the Flood" is much superior in vividness and intelligibility. Here his imagination was at work on the material provided by the story in Genesis, modifying it and adding to it. It is his one surviving attempt to use Scots in poetry. It has greater verbal vitality than the other ballad, and this makes one wish that he had used Scots more often. It may be that he was led to the subject by its suitability to his own condition—he had escaped to firm ground, having been in danger of being overwhelmed by the flood welling up from his own subconscious; but any such personal meaning that the story may have had for him is rightly not obtruded. At this stage he was able to write better when working on material given by history or myth than when trying to deal with his personal problems directly.

In three poems—"When the Trees grow bare," "Autumn in Prague" and "October in Hellbrünn"—he seeks to evoke a mood, to define a state of being, not by use of myth but by the description of a natural scene. The mood is one of calm and at the same time of exhaustion, and is presumably symptomatic of the state in which recovery from his neurosis at first left him. "Betrayal" presents the image of beauty caught in the snare of time—a favourite idea with Muir, but here treated in rather an obvious and banal way.

His next poem, a long one, *Chorus of the Newly Dead* (1926) was written, or at any rate begun, in the spring and summer of 1924 in Austria. Walking in the woods he felt the stirrings of the new poem,

> a chorus in which the dead were to look back at the life they had left and contemplate it from their new station. The idea greatly moved me, but my imaginative excitement never managed to communicate itself, or at best now and then, to the poem; the old disability which I had struggled with at Hellerau, a simple lack of skill, still held me up. In any case the theme was far too great for my powers.[7]

The poem was never reprinted, though in two copies of it Muir made sustained efforts to revise it. In one all the choruses except the first and last are deleted, as is the harlot's speech; some of the other speeches are considerably revised. He must have thought the poem worth working on, but was not able to bring it to a state which satisfied him.

The newly dead are the idiot, the beggar, the coward, the harlot, the poet and the mystic. Each speaks of his life on earth from his new standpoint among the dead, and after each the chorus meditates on the significance of that life. From his new freedom Muir was reconstructing the cramped life he had lived and had seen others live in Glasgow, and was trying to see meaning in those lives. There is a compassionate awareness of suffering and evil; and no easy answer is given to the problems posed by them:

> We cannot tell
> Why harlot idiot or clown
> Lived, wept and died.[8]

But in the mystic's contribution and in the final chorus there is an attempt to see everything as contained in a permanent pattern:

> That stationary country where
>   Achilles drives and Hector runs,
> Making a movement in the air
>   Forever, under all the suns!
>
> And that ghostly eternity
>   Cut by the bridge where journeys Christ,
> On endless arcs pacing the sea,
>   Time turning with his solar tryst![9]

Reading these lines thirty years later Muir found them very strange, as if they had been written by someone else. But the theme—the paradox of permanence and change —remained one of his central ones. Perhaps the strangeness for him lay in the fact that in them the Nietzschean influence is still strong. As yet neither the thought nor the images in which it is expressed are altogether clear.

Variations on a Time Theme (1934) followed after a long interval. Mr Hall included only four of its ten sections in the 1952 collection, but Muir restored the full text in 1960, implying, however, that he agreed with Mr Hall's judgment. The inferiority of some of the early poems having been acknowledged by their exclusion, it was now possible to put them back because "they express certain things which I wanted to say at the time and have not said in the same way again."[10] We may take it, therefore, that Muir was not altogether satisfied with the *Variations* as a whole.

They should be read as a series of meditations on a theme rather than as a continuous long poem. The most illuminating comment is Muir's own on the second section, which was first published separately under the title of "The Riders." He wrote to Miss Gwendolen Murphy, when she was compiling her anthology, *The Modern Poet*:

The point round which the poem crystallised was the
beginning:

> At the dead centre of the boundless plain
> Does our way end? Our horses pace and pace
> Like steeds forever labouring on a shield.

These lines came to me spontaneously, without my
being conscious of the possible development they im-
plied. The development grew from a variety of associations that would have remained isolated and
disconnected but for this image, which acted as a sort
of magnet, and drew them into a rough pattern round
it. The Horses, as I see them, are an image of human
time, the invisible body of humanity on which we ride
for a little while, which has come from places we do
not know:

> They have borne upon their saddles
> Forms fiercer than the tiger, borne them calmly
> As they bear us now,

And which is going towards places we shall not know:

> Suppliantly
> The rocks will melt, the sealed horizons fall
> Before their onset.

Yet the steed—mankind in its course through time—is
mortal, and the rider is immortal. I stated this belief
tentatively in the poem, because it was written in a
mood of unusual dejection. The painful emotion in
the poem comes from a simultaneous feeling of immortality and mortality, and particularly from the
feeling that we, as immortal spirits, are imprisoned
in a very small and from all appearances fortuitously
selected length of time: held captive on the "worn
saddle" which in spite of our belief in our immortality
has the power "to charm us to obliviousness" by "the
scent of the ancient leather."

I was not aware, or at least fully aware, of all these implications when I wrote the poem; and I have only realised during the last year that almost all my poems from the start have been about journeys and places: that is about the two sides of the paradox one of which implies the other.[11]

Miss Murphy asked him about the autumn light in the lines:

> And so we do not hope
> That their great coal-black glossy hides
> Should keep a glimmer of the autumn light
> We still remember, when our limbs were weightless
> As red leaves on a tree, and our silvery breaths
> Went on before us like new-risen souls
> Leading our empty bodies through the air.[12]

He answered:

I actually saw once, many years ago, the picture as I set it down: it is one of the few things in the poem taken from observation. It was a clear bright day in late autumn down in Sussex: the weight seemed to have left every physical object with the drying up of the leaves still sticking to the trees without burdening them. A boy was ploughing in a field, and a moving column of breath went on before him; his own breath; but the air was so light and clear, the picture so distinct, that what my eye saw was the column going in front and the boy following it. Why this struck me so much I can't say yet; but when I came to this part of the poem it seemed to be the correspondence I needed.

". . . The autumn light / We still remember" of which the "coal-black glossy hides" do not keep a glimmer. I think this is an attempt to suggest those isolated moments of pure vision which have a feeling of

timelessness (and are often called timeless). My feeling
about these moments (which are a common experience,
though most people are unconscious of them) has
always been that they do not *go into* Time; that they
do not change the actual physical body of Time,
symbolised by the horses. They may cast a momentary
reflection on the glossy hides, but it fades almost at
once. This instant fading makes them "autumnal".
At the moment when we are aware of them we are
released from the presence of Time: our limbs are
"weightless". Our silvery breaths going on before us
"Leading our empty bodies through the air" is an
extravagant way of describing this state of freedom.[13]

This is very interesting, but it may be objected that the
poem should not need all this explaining—or at least that
the explanation should do no more than point to meanings which are really there in the words. Are they? In
general, in this poem—one of the best of the *Variations*—
they are. But in some of the other sections the writing is
so compressed as to be obscure, as in the final one. The
thought is not always incarnated satisfactorily in the
images. There are interesting thoughts, and images in
themselves striking; the two are not always fused.

The central theme is the paradoxical co-existence in us
of the consciousness of mortality and of immortality, of
the feeling of being imprisoned within a fore-ordained
course in a short length of time and of the occasional
feeling of freedom and timelessness. The individual's
descent from Eden into the wilderness of time is, as in
The Story and the Fable, connected with the fall of mankind. The journey is at once that of each individual and
that of the race.

One of the best sections is No. VI,[14] in which the
general theme is made real to the imagination in a
description of the journey of the children of Israel
through the wilderness:

E

> Forty years this burning
> Circuitous path, feet spurning
> The sliding sand and turning
> 　The wheel, turning again
> Sharp rock, soft dust, a land
> 　Choked in sand.

Their way continues circuitously through the wastes without apparent aim; but there are moments when a superior reality makes itself known—in the stream smitten from the rock and in Jehovah's coming to Mount Sinai. The too close approach of the supernatural is feared, and the Israelites turn from it, making "a golden toy" and shattering the peace with their dancing. So they must go on through the wilderness, almost losing their memories of "something once tender and green." Yet they know that there is a goal, and a way to it, and that they will reach it:

> There is a stream
> We have been told of. Where it is
> We do not know. But it is not a dream,
> Though like a dream. We cannot miss
> The road that leads us to it. Fate
> Will take us there that keeps us here.

The theme is more successfully embodied in the poetry here than in those sections in which ideas are meditated on in a more abstract way. The use of a known story enables the meaning to be grasped more easily than when a private myth is used.

Journeys and Places (1937) was Muir's first book of detached short poems since 1925, except that six of the items in it had been printed in a fine limited edition in 1932. So the volume contains the work of quite a long period, and is rather uneven in quality. Nine of the original twenty-five poems were excluded from the 1952 collection; all but one, "Saul," were restored in 1960.

In these poems Muir is preoccupied with the same

problems as in *Variations on a Time Theme*. Man is bound
to time, but has intuitions of eternity. He journeys along
turning roads through mountainous country. Behind the
past recedes into the mists of memory, and he cannot
find his way back to it. In front he sees "futurity's high-
walled land," but he is confined to the present and must
continue along the turning roads. He does not know for
certain which road is the right one; and sometimes the
roads have a Kafkaesque perversity in seeming to lead
no nearer to a goal. Yet he feels an assurance that his
apparently wandering journey will be seen in the end
to have had a pattern. He dreams

> of a peak whose height
> Will show me every hill,
> A single mountain on whose side
> Life blooms for ever and is still.[15]

He has a vision of hills on which

> The gods reclined and conversed with each other
> From summit to summit.

The vision fades, but there remains

> The living dream sprung from the dying vision,
> Overarching all. Beneath its branches
> He builds in faith and doubt his shaking house.[16]

This last line is characteristically tentative. He is seeking
for a way to reconcile the apparent opposites—time and
eternity, necessity and freedom; but he does not yet see
clearly how to do so.

The thought as embodied in the poems is, of course,
much more subtle, complex, and interesting than a summary can suggest. The poems are not, except in some
weaker parts, versified speculations. They do not usually
take their origin from a train of thought, which the poet
then seeks images to express, but rather from an experience. As we have seen, "The Riders" originated

from an image, which came to Muir spontaneously; associations clustered round this image, and the poet himself only gradually became aware of its possible implications. Some of the poems in *Journeys and Places* probably began in the same way; others started from dreams or from things seen or read about which excited the poet's imagination. We should start by seeing what he shows us, and entering into the feeling of the poems.

In a prefatory note Muir explained:

The Journeys and Places in this collection should be taken as having a rough-and-ready psychological connotation rather than a strict temporal or spatial one. The first deal more or less with movements in time, and the second with places reached and the character of such places; but I have also included in the latter division imaginary situations which by a licence of the fancy may perhaps pass as places, that is as pauses in time.[17]

The object in this kind of poetry is to describe not—or not usually—actual scenes, but visionary landscapes having some symbolic meaning. It is essential that the images should both embody the thought and feeling to be expressed and be in themselves vivid to the imagination. Not all these poems fulfil equally well both these requirements. Sometimes, in his anxiety to make his meaning clear, Muir expresses it too abstractly instead of embodying it in images so as to convey it in a truly poetic way. Sometimes, on the other hand, the images are in themselves vivid, but one does not at first know what to make of them. This second situation is less destructive to the success of the poetry than the first, and a reader with a little patience will seldom find that he cannot feel his way towards an understanding of Muir's never wilfully difficult symbolism.

Comparing *The Sufficient Place*[18] with the later poem

based on a dream, *The Combat*, one can see how far Muir
had yet to go towards making his vision real in word
and image. What he was trying to convey in the earlier
poem is plain enough. It is based on memories of his
childhood home in Orkney and on some later occasions
when he experienced again something of the old feeling
of peace and security. Once in a dream he seemed to be
re-visiting his old home as an old man, and he saw it
surrounded by thick, still trees very much as the sufficient
place is described in the poem;[19] once in Italy he and
some friends visited a peasant family in a remote place,
and were treated with a ceremonious courtesy which
made him "dimly aware of a good life which had existed
there for many centuries";[20] and later in Orkney he
stayed in a farmhouse where the serenity of the life
reminded him of the Italian family.[21] It is the dream
which has had most influence on the poem. Muir
describes not any actual place—not his own home, nor
the Italian peasant's, nor the Orkney farmer's—but the
little house as seen in the dream; and the Man and
Woman are not individualised, but left as archetypal
figures. The only lines which bring the scene in any
detail before one's eyes are those on the tall trees, so
thick-leaved that there seems hardly room for the birds
to sit on the boughs. (Remembering the comparative
treelessness of Orkney one appreciates what this vision
would mean to Muir; it suggests richness, fullness of
life, fertility, as well as peace and security.) The interior
of the house is not described visually at all. The room is
like, not any material thing, but "a thought which
needed thus much space to write on." All this is done
deliberately. Muir wants to describe a place glimpsed
in dreams and in real life—to which some actual homes
may approximate, but which is a pattern, not any particular place in the world. It is a state of being, which
different people have experienced under different conditions; and so it is, perhaps, appropriate to allow each

reader to fill in the details for himself. The poem has a
calm, grave beauty, especially in the opening and closing
lines, and will appeal powerfully to anyone who has had
experiences similar to those which lie behind it; but I am
not sure that it has throughout sufficient vitality in its
language and imagery to convey these experiences very
strongly to those for whom they are remote. Perhaps, in
the middle lines especially, Muir is relying too much on
what a sympathetic reader will be able to put in.

There is no difficulty in understanding the meaning of
the sufficient place—it is quite clearly stated in the poem;
the doubt is whether it is conveyed in a sufficiently com-
pelling way to the imagination. A different question
arises in connexion with "The Enchanted Knight":

Lulled by La Belle Dame Sans Merci he lies
  In the bare wood below the blackening hill.
The plough drives nearer now, the shadow flies
  Past him across the plain, but he lies still.

Long since the rust its gardens here have planned,
  Flowering his armour like an autumn field.
From his sharp breast-plate to his iron hand
  A spider's web is stretched, a phantom shield.

When footsteps pound the turf beside his ear
  Armies pass through his dream in endless line,
And one by one his ancient friends appear;
  They pass all day, but he can make no sign.

When a bird cries within the silent grove
  The long-lost voice goes by, he makes to rise
And follow, but his cold limbs never move,
  And on the turf unstirred his shadow lies.

But if a withered leaf should drift
  Across his face and rest, the dread drops start
Chill on his forehead. Now he tries to lift
  The insulting weight that stays and breaks his heart.[22]

Here the scene is certainly made real to the imagination
and the senses of the reader. The touches of precise detail
in the description—the blackening hill, the spider's web,
the withered leaf lying on the knight's face—are sufficient
without being too many. The last stanza conveys well a
feeling of immobility and strain. The poet here succeeds
in making us see and feel as he intends. The words may
not, perhaps, be individually very striking, but some of
them in their contexts carry a considerable weight of
meaning—*e.g.*, "The *insulting* weight that stays and
breaks his heart." A complex image that appeals to
one's imagination is certainly created in this poem.
Many will be content to leave it at that, and simply to
enjoy the enchanted scene. Others may confess at first to
a state of bewilderment, and ask what the poem "means."
Of course one should not expect to be able to give a
simple, clearly-defined answer to such a question; this is
not allegory. But, remembering Muir's own note on the
journeys and places in this volume, one may legitimately
try to make clear to oneself what psychological "place"
the knight occupies. One can, if one likes, relate the
knight's situation to common, and to Muir's, experience,
though after all attempts at explanation there will remain, quite properly, a sense of mystery, of strangeness.
He is caught in a sort of death-in-life; the ordinary
activities of life go on around him, but he is unable to
join in them; he dreams of his comrades going out to
battle, but he cannot join in the work proper to him as a
knight. He is alienated from the world of action, but is
still in some way aware of it. Something like this is quite
common in dreams. One has a despairing sense of
helplessness and immobility, while knowing that some
action is urgently necessary; one's limbs or one's tongue
will not obey one; the feeling is similar to that conveyed
by the last stanza of the poem. I suppose such dreams
correspond in waking life to the sense of alienation from
one's surroundings and from other people that occurs in

some neuroses, and, in less extreme forms, in more ordinary conditions. Muir had known this sense of alienation as a child (during his time of irrational fear connected with the sheep dip) and in the later Glasgow days. More immediately relevant here may be the sense of exhaustion which his neurosis seems to have left with him after he had begun to recover from it and which is reflected in some of *First Poems*. One of the poems in that volume, which were later rejected is "The Enchanted Prince," of which "The Enchanted Knight" is a much more effective re-working. More recently, as the letters from France to Mr and Mrs Thorburn, quoted earlier, showed, Muir had felt cut off as a man of letters from the practical activities of his Glasgow friends. Many writers feel like this at times, regret that they are mere spectators, and wish, like Yeats, that they could prove their worth in "something all others understand and share." Thinking along these lines, one could identify La Belle Dame as the Muse, who lures her devotees away from ordinary life and uses up all their energies. Of course, no such simple interpretation is adequate. Muir may well not have known himself precisely why the scene he imagined appealed to him; and it is not necessary to bring in any knowledge of his life in order to respond to it. The poem acts on the reader's imagination, not only because the scene it presents is clearly visualised, but also because it suggests a spiritual state, of alienation, which in various forms and induced by various causes is not uncommon.

These are both good poems, especially the second, but not among his very best. Later he was to be able to bring together more perfectly thought, feeling, and sensuous impressions. His progress was towards a clearer and more comprehensive vision, and towards a greater mastery of the art of embodying his thought in imagery.

In concentrating on these two poems I have failed to do justice to the variety of *Journeys and Places*; not all the

poems in it deal with dream-like experiences, nor with
Muir's personal myth. He was still concerned mainly to
write his own fable, to understand the meaning of his
own life. But even in order to do these things he needed
to look away from himself and relate his experiences to
those of others. One of his best early poems had been
"Ballad of Hector in Hades," in which he had been able
to release himself from a terrifying event in his own past
by objectifying it. Even in that poem the protagonist had
been really himself. But now his imagination is excited
by incidents and situations, found in literature and history, not always related so closely to his own life. The
range of his vision is growing. After his own "Mythical
Journey" we find "Tristram's Journey" and "Hölderlin's
Journey"; and over a third of the "places" are dramatic
—the protagonist is someone other than himself. This
was a good augury for the future. If he had been able to
do nothing but look back and till over and over again the
small field of his childhood memories, his inspiration
would surely, like Wordsworth's, have dried up. He was
to show himself able to assimilate new experiences as
well as to achieve clearer understanding of past ones, to
look out at the world around him and to apprehend the
patterns, revealed in myth, which underlie history.

REFERENCES

1. *A.*, p. 205.
2. *A.*, p. 206.
3. *C.P.*, p. 19.
4. *C.P.*, p. 20.
5. *A.*, p. 206.
6. *A.*, pp. 159–63, 165–7.
7. *A.*, p. 223.
8. *C.N.D.*, p. 10.
9. *C.N.D.*, p. 15.
10. *C.P.*, p. 7.
11. *The Modern Poet: An Anthology* (1938), pp. 168–9.
12. *C.P.*, p. 41.
13. *Modern Poet*, pp. 169–70.
14. *C.P.*, pp. 45–7.
15. "The Mountains," in *C.P.*, pp. 59–60.
16. "The Mythical Journey," in *C.P.*, p. 63.
17. *Journeys and Places*, p. viii.
18. *C.P.*, pp. 86–7.
19. *A.*, pp. 64–5.
20. *A.*, p. 212.
21. *A.*, p. 241.
22. *C.P.*, p. 74.

CHAPTER V

THE POET: II

The Narrow Place (1943) shows an advance on what had gone before both in skill and in range. There is a greater mastery of a variety of metrical forms and of rhythmical effects. For instance, "The Day" consists of one long, perfectly clear and logical sentence, fitted without apparent strain into seventeen lines of rhyming decasyllabic verse; and in "The Old Gods" a difficult rhyme-scheme is handled with great skill. The rhythm is usually slow and grave, suited to Muir's reflective kind of poetry; but in "The Bird" he tries something rather unusual for him, making the movement of the verse suggest the bird's flight. There is also greater variety of subject than before. Only two poems return to childhood memories; a few others deal directly with more recent experiences of his own. But in most of the poems he looks outside himself—at Scottish history, at the War, at some philosophical or religious theme. These categories, of course, are not absolutely distinct; in some of the best poems personal, political, philosophical, and religious themes are combined. Above all this volume is superior to its predecessors in the greater ability Muir shows in it to bring together ideas and the description of actual or imagined scenes, to achieve a completer fusion of image and theme.

This last point can be illustrated in "The Return of Odysseus."[1] Here we have, not a landscape of dream as in "The Sufficient Place," but a place which might exist in the every-day world:

The doors flapped open in Odysseus' house,
The lolling latches gave to every hand,
Let traitor, babbler, tout and bargainer in.
The rooms and passages resounded
With ease and chaos of a public market,
The walls mere walls to lean on as you talked,
Spat on the floor, surveyed some newcomer
With an absent eye. There you could be yourself.

The anarchy which is threatening to destroy the good
order of Odysseus' home during his long absence is made
real in the precise images of the flapping doors and the
lolling latches. In the midst of the disorder "at the
house's heart . . . in a clean room" Penelope sits faith-
fully at her task, the seemingly futile one of weaving and
unweaving her wedding garment, and thereby keeps the
suitors at bay. Sometimes she wonders whether it is
worth while. Will Odysseus ever return? But:

Odysseus, this is duty,
To do and undo, to keep a vacant gate
Where order and right and hope and peace can enter.

As she weaves, though she does not know it

Odysseus on the long
And winding road of the world was on his way.

There is some falling off in actuality at the end here, and
it was, perhaps, unwise to let Penelope make the large
claim for herself. Muir may have felt this; for he returned
to the theme later, and put the story into the mouth of
Telemachos, who vividly describes his mother's task, one
which as a boy he had not understood

Not knowing she wove into her fears
Pride and fidelity and love.[2]

In both poems, especially the second, Muir earns his
right to use the large abstract words and gives them

definite meaning, because the poems as wholes are not
too abstract. In the first part of the earlier poem and in
the whole of the second (which is also more complex
and wider-ranging in meaning) the larger significances
he sees in the story are well embodied in the descriptions.

"The Return of Odysseus" describes an imagined
scene in a realistic way; "The Wayside Station"[3]
describes an actual one:

> Here at the wayside station, as many a morning,
> I watch the smoke torn from the fumy engine
> Curling across the field in serpent sorrow.
> Flat in the east, held down by stolid clouds,
> The struggling day is born and shines already
> On its warm hearth far off. Yet something here
> Glimmers along the ground to show the seagulls
> White on the furrows' black unturning waves.

The light broadens as he watches a farmstead on a little
hill, and thinks of the cattle, the ploughboy and the
farmer waking, and of lovers parting; the branches of
the trees are lit to dark silver (it is, presumably, winter)
and

>   The lonely stream
> That rode through darkness leaps the gap of light,
> Its voice grown loud, and starts its winding journey
> Through the day and time and war and history.

After the concrete descriptions of familiar things the last
line with its large general terms is unexpected. Suddenly
the horizon is widened, and the small familiar things are
seen in a wider context, both of space and time. Here, as
in "The Return of Odysseus," a single line of abstract
words is effectively introduced after concrete and precise
images. The poem has been said to be uncharacteristic
of Muir in being merely descriptive; but it is not so. The
scene is not only described; it is endowed with significance. In some ways similar is "The River,"[4] written

"soon after the invasion of France, which brought images of universal disaster to so many of us. Frontier walls seemed to be beyond saving just then, and I had an image of Europe quite featureless, with all the old marks gone."[5] The river can be imagined as any actual river flowing through war-time Europe past blackened fields, bombed towns and refugee crowds. It can also be understood as an image of history flowing through time. In either case the question asked is whether, in space or time, there is any pattern, any meaning. Is history a meaningless flux leading to no destination? It seems so:

> The stream
> Runs on into the day of time and Europe,
> Past the familiar walls and friendly roads,
> Now thronged with dumb migrations, gods and altars
> That travel towards no destination. Then
> The disciplined soldiers come to conquer nothing,
> March upon emptiness and do not know
> Why all is dead and life has hidden itself.
> The enormous winding frontier walls fall down,
> Leaving anonymous stone and vacant grass.

And yet, in the closing lines another possibility is suggested—characteristically in the form of a question:

> The stream flows on into what land, what peace,
> Far past the other side of the burning world?

Again a wider horizon is suddenly revealed in the final lines. It may be thought that too much reliance is placed on the effect of the single word "peace" here; but in the context the quietness of the last two lines is perfectly right. The main effect of the poem is intended to be to bring before us vividly images of destruction; these were what were filling the mind at the time. The note of hope is intended to be sounded only in a muted, tentative way.

These poems and others in which the thought is embodied in a clearly visualised scene or story are those which are likely to appeal most immediately to a new

reader of Muir. Others that make an immediate appeal
are those which express quite simply and directly personal experience—such as "The Day" and the love-
poem, "The Confirmation." The poems in which the
thought is expressed more abstractly or by the use of a
succession of images rather than by the development of
a single one are more difficult to get into, but most of
them repay careful reading. His central themes are still
the same—time and eternity, necessity and freedom. In
"The Recurrence" he denies Nietzsche's theory that all
things return in a fated order. Admittedly what the eye
sees is the wheel of necessity; events seem to succeed one
another in a strict chain of cause and effect. But the heart
and the mind know a different order in which each
moment is new, in which there is creation. In a deter-
ministic universe there would be no place for God, but
God's presence and activity within time mean that there
is a possibility of freedom for man. Muir is now giving
more precise and more specifically religious answers to
the questions that he raises. Before he had been able to
say only that man has intuitions both of necessity and of
freedom; now he is able to go some way towards explaining the paradox (though without removing a sense
of mystery), and towards showing why the intuition of
freedom is justified. In "The Wheel"[6] the order opposed to that of fate is specifically identified as that of
grace:

> Nothing can come of history but history,
> The stationary storm that cannot bate
> Its neutral violence . . .
> Unless a grace
> Come of itself to wrap our souls in peace
> Between the turning wheel of history and make
> Ourselves ourselves, winnow the grudging grain,
> And take
> From that which made us that which will make us
>   again.

The central idea is a familiar one, but it is here given new life and meaning by the vitality of the diction and imagery ("stationary storm," "neutral violence," "grudging grain."). A similar thought is expressed more dramatically in the meditations of the dying Bruce in "Robert the Bruce."[7] As he thinks of his murder of Comyn, Bruce sees that in the order of fate he can never be released from that act. If there is nothing but an endless chain of cause and effect, no action is either good or bad; the past need not be regretted, and cannot be redeemed; there can be no forgiveness:

> "But that Christ hung upon the Cross,
>   Comyn would rot until time's end
> And bury my sin in boundless dust,
>   For there is no amend
>
> In order; yet in order run
>   All things by unreturning ways.
> If Christ live not, nothing is here
>   For sorrow or for praise."

In both these poems Muir is carefully honest in not expressing a greater confidence than he feels. "Unless a grace come . . ."; "But that Christ hung . . .". The conditional mood is used. Nothing is stated dogmatically. Though his faith in the possibility of an order of grace was growing, he was still at times possessed by the anti-vision of men, including himself, as nothing but animals. "Then" expresses a nightmare vision of primitive savagery; in "The Face" he looks beneath the deceptively "untroubled oval" of his own face to the evil and destructive passions he finds within himself; in "The Refugees" he deals with the ultimately self-destroying indifference with which men contemplate the sufferings of others; and in "Scotland 1941" he writes bitterly of the forces which have divided the Scottish nation and corrupted her culture. The poems in which the note of hope is struck are all the more impressive for the realism of those in which the power of evil and the difficulty of faith are acknowledged.

The Narrow Place shows Muir stretching out from his world of dreams, from a preoccupation with his own subjective states, to incorporate more and more of the actual world, both present and past, within the scope of his vision.

The next volume, *The Voyage* (1946), shows a yet further advance in Muir's mastery of his medium. This can be seen, for instance, in the four sonnets, which are made up largely of longish sentences, which run quite naturally and with apparent ease while conforming to the difficult verse pattern. He reminds us of George Herbert in his capacity to talk in verse. He can sing, too, when he wants to. More characteristically, however, he speaks to us, using the ordinary constructions and word order of prose, but in a voice which has the rhythm and the intensity of poetry. He reminds us of Herbert, too, by his tone of uncomplacent serenity. He is humble about himself, clear-eyed about the state of the world, and still suffers moods of depression. But now in late middle-age his predominant mood—attained not easily, but by spiritual effort—is of acceptance and gratitude. He has got back to something like the old paradisal feeling; but it is not the same—the new serenity contains the wisdom won from experience.

This volume gives expression to many different moods and thoughts and experiences, but I will confine myself here to the last six poems in it, which beautifully express Muir's recovery of the lost Eden. "The Transmutation" must be read in association with those earlier poems in which he had conveyed a nightmare sense of being confined within time, his fear that there might be "no crack or chink, no escape from Time."[8] He had feared either that there was no permanence, but only a meaningless succession of events, or that, if there were any perma-

F

nence, it was only the permanence of Nietzsche's eternal recurrence. He had for long had the contrary intuition that there is an escape, and recently had come to feel that the key to the mystery lay in Christianity. But never before had he expressed with such wondering confidence the actual experience of finding the escape he had sought. Time, he knows now, is not a closed circle; we do "fall through time's long ruin," and are able out of events in time to weave a permanent pattern in its borders. The permanence is not a mere repetition in which the past can never be redeemed. There is transmutation.

The next poem, "Time Held in Time's Despite," develops the same theme in a more personal way. Love is one of the agents of transmutation. He and his wife have been able in time to make something of their own, which transcends time and will outlast it:

> The hours that melt like snowflakes one by one
> Leave us this residue, this virgin ground
> For ever fresh, this firmament and this sun.
>
> Then let us lay unasking hand in hand,
> And take our way, thus led, into our land.

The next poem, "For Ann Scott-Moncrieff," read by itself might seem to be merely a tribute to a friend who had died young. Reading it in its context we see that it is that, and something more; for it continues the meditation on what may be built in time "in time's despite." Not only by love can something good and whole be made, but also by courage and honesty in the ordinary course of living, especially in face of suffering. The dead girl had suffered in life, like others, from "ills of body and soul"; "smashed to bits by the Fall," she had striven to make herself whole, to become more truly herself. Now, in death, she is "entirely Ann."

Next, in "A Birthday," recovered Eden is seen in a renewed delight in, and sense of oneness with, nature.

This at-oneness Muir had felt as a child, lost as a boy and young man, and had been gradually recovering since 1922. Now he is able to feel more vividly than ever before

> The tingling smell and touch
> Of dogrose and sweet briar,

and to accept with gratitude not only the sweets, but the sours also, to look back with gratitude over the whole course of his life.

"All We" is another variation on the theme of building something good out of the transitory. As the married lovers in one way, as Ann Scott-Moncrieff in another, so also in their own way "all we," the artists, do the same thing. Artists (and indeed all who try to make something shapely) know

> the delicacy
> Of bringing shape to birth

and are able to take special pleasure in the Maker's solicitude and artistry in His creation. In creation, both God's and the artist's, time and eternity are reconciled, married:

> To fashion the transitory
> We gave and took the ring
> And pledged ourselves to the earth.

These poems are variations on a theme, but do not repeat themselves. Each adds something new. The thought moves from a general statement on transmutation through a number of particular, and quite different, examples of how that transmutation occurs—in love, in moral effort, in response to natural beauty, in artistic creation. After reading the five poems we see that we must be careful not to misrepresent Muir in saying that he sought and found an "escape from time" (though he uses the phrase himself). It is not so much an escape from time that he finds as an escape from the conception of time as a closed circle. It is not by dreaming of another world that he finds salvation, but by a profounder vision of what goes on in this one. The final poem, "In Love for Long," does not really contradict this, though at first it may seem to:

> I've been in love for long
> With what I cannot tell
> And will contrive a song
> For the intangible. . . .
>
> This happy happy love
> Is sieged with crying sorrows,
> Crushed beneath and above
> Between to-days and morrows;
> A little paradise
> Held in the world's vice.
>
> And there it is content
> And careless as a child,
> And in imprisonment
> Flourishes sweet and wild;
> In wrong, beyond wrong,
> All the world's day long.

His love is ultimately for something which is intangible and beyond time, but yet it is content within the world's vice and flourishes in imprisonment. This love is not opposed to the love of particular persons and tangible things expressed in the earlier poems.

In this group of poems we find a sense of recovered wholeness—both within himself and between himself and people and things. This harmony is reflected in the writing, which has a beautiful simplicity and clarity.

Reading those final serene poems in *The Voyage* in 1946 one's delight might well have been tinged with fear lest the poet had come to port at the end of his voyage, had mastered his conflicts, and so might have no more to say. One would not have had to read far in the next volume, *The Labyrinth* (1949), to have this fear removed. For this, produced when Muir was over sixty, is probably his finest volume, containing some of his greatest poems and displaying the most consistently high level of accomplishment. It is the first and only one none of whose contents were excluded from either of the collected editions. A good many of the poems are retrospective. Muir felt the need to look back at the whole of his journey through the labyrinth of time, and to interpret in the light of his mature wisdom the fable which he saw beneath the story. In some poems he speaks in his own person; in others the speaker is some character from myth or history or from imagination. Similar patterns are seen in these other lives to those which he had found in his own. But the poems are not repetitive. Different aspects of the fable of man are illustrated in the different lives.

Muir was not always looking into the past, however. As an old man he showed a remarkable capacity to assimilate new experiences and to relate them to old. And he was not always concerned with himself. He was deeply affected by what he saw in Europe between 1945 and 1948, and some fine poems grew out of his experiences there.

In the title poem[9] both the old nightmare of imprisonment within a closed world and the contrary vision of peace and freedom are given more eloquent expression than ever before. The protagonist is Theseus, who, as a young man, volunteered to be one of the party of seven youths and seven maidens paid in tribute by Athens to Crete to be fed to the Minotaur, half-human half-bull, who lived in the centre of the maze; helped by Ariadne, he slew the Minotaur and escaped. Muir modifies the myth to suit himself. In the poem Theseus seems to be alone and unaided; there is no mention of him following

a thread supplied by someone else; what he slays is
simply "the bull." One should begin, not by trying to
explain the symbolism to oneself, but by responding to
the rhythms and images, the touches of detail, which
enable one to share the hero's experience.

> After the straw ceased rustling and the bull
> Lay dead . . .

in trying to get out he was

> Dazed with the tall and echoing passages,
> The swift recoils, so many I almost feared
> I'd meet myself returning at some smooth corner. . . .

However, he did get out, and at first stared in wonder at
the bright world around him. Since then there have been
times when he has heard his footsteps "still echoing in
the maze," when the whole world has seemed to be one
great Labyrinth from which there is no exit (all this is
told in a single, labyrinthine sentence of thirty-four and
a half lines—a remarkable *tour de force*). One voice
within him tells him that he is free—"all roads lie free
before you"; but another sneers:

> 'Haste and delay are equal
> In this one world, for there's no exit, none,
> No place to come to, and you'll end where you are,
> Deep in the centre of the endless maze.'

In the final meditation he rejects this second view—not
by argument, but by presenting a vision of the gods

> Each sitting on the top of his mountain-isle

and conversing across the sounds in tranquil voices, while
below the ordinary life of men goes on, "all permissible,
all acceptable,"

> And their eternal dialogue was peace
> Where all these things were woven, and this our life
> Was as a chord deep in that dialogue.

He has had this vision once, and the memory of it suffices to reassure him, even though the dream of imprisonment within the Labyrinth returns.

This is a new version of the old dialogue between determinism and freedom. Determinism is an illusion, a lie, though a powerful one; the vision of freedom is a vision of the real world. Ultimately time and eternity are not opposed; for the ordinary life of men is woven into the eternal dialogue of the gods. But no single explanation exhausts the meaning of the symbolism. One can think of the Labyrinth as the whole realm of time which shuts men out from a perception of eternity; but primarily here it is what Blake calls the selfhood. In "The Transfiguration," in the presence of Christ, murderers

> And those who hide within the labyrinth
> Of their own loneliness and greatness came,
> And those entangled in their own devices, . . .
> Stepped out of their dungeons and were free.[10]

To be in the Labyrinth is to be enclosed in oneself. But perhaps, too, it is necessary, especially for the poet, to descend into the Labyrinth (in one aspect, his own subconscious?) in order, having ascended from it, to attain to vision.

Theseus' experiences can also be related specifically to Muir's own. The time in the Labyrinth may be said to correspond to his long illness in Glasgow and his near-breakdown afterwards. In Glasgow he had feared that he might be engulfed for ever among the slums (the phrase "the tall and echoing passages" is rather unexpected as applied to the maze, but is appropriate to streets of high tenements); he had felt a sense of alienation from the natural world, and in his neurosis had been near to a disintegration of personality in which he might have feared to meet himself (which would have been a sign of that disintegration having taken place). The escape from the Labyrinth can be related to his recovery of health of mind in the early nineteen-twenties—a recovery which did not preclude the return of periods of depression in which not Glasgow alone, not any particular place alone, but the whole world seemed a maze of roads leading to no end and from which there might be no escape. The vision of peace at the end is of an idealised peasant community living on a group of islands, and inevitably reminds us of the Orkneys. So the poem includes autobiographical elements. But it is not just a symbolic way of telling the story of the poet's life, nor just a symbolic way of considering a philosophical problem. It presents a myth, which can be applied in several ways, in which each reader can see something of his own life and which has a vitality of its own.

"The Labyrinth" gives most attention to the nightmare, though the escape from it is also shown. Another poem in the same volume, "The Transfiguration,"[11] attempts, not quite so successfully, to convey a feeling of the experience diametrically opposite to that of imprisonment within the self. Like several other late ones of Muir's, this poem contains a new and more complete statement of a theme he had often touched on before. He had experienced, most clearly in dreams but also in real life, moments in which people and things had appeared to him transfigured. One such had been during his first May Day parade in Glasgow. What he remembered most clearly about that day was that "all distinction had fallen away like a burden carried in another place, and that all substance had been transmuted."[12] In normal life we cannot help making distinctions, being aware that some people are wise and some foolish, some clean and some dirty, etc.; but in some special moments such distinctions are either not seen or appear unimportant; all mankind seem "made of some incorruptible substance," and no disgust nor repugnance is felt for ugliness or disease. Such moments came to

Muir more often in dreams than in life. In one dream
he saw a great crystal river, in which multitudes of
people of more than life size were bathing, a river which
"could easily wash away every impurity and still remain
pure."[13] In another he was woken by a robed figure, who
took him through moonlit streets into a field. On the way
they met a shabby blood-stained man, whom he took to
be a murderer, and of whom he was afraid, until he saw
his look of adoration for the robed man. The crowd of
ragged people they met all had this same look of adoration in their eyes. In the field all these and a host of
animals joined in a solemn and mysterious act of wor-
ship. It was a dream of the Millennium. So, for Muir,
the story of the Transfiguration was not about something
remote from normal experience, which Christians believe happened on an unique occasion; it was an example
of a way of seeing which he had, in lesser ways, known as
a fact of experience. The Transfiguration, as he describes
it through the mouths of the Disciples, is really a re-
creation of his millennial dream rather than of the
Biblical narrative. It is not about the Transfiguration of
Christ at all, but about the transfiguration of all things
in His presence. The Disciples' sight is cleansed and they
experience a moment in which is given back to them
"the clear unfallen world"; afterwards the ordinary
world rolls back, and "the radiant kingdom" is no more
seen, but they believe it is still there:

> alone it flowers and shines
> And blossoms for itself while time runs on.

It *blossoms*; the present tense is used. The rediscovery of
Eden is made here not by returning into the past nor by
dreaming of the future, but by a sharpening of the sight
to see a permanent reality that underlies time. But even
here he characteristically allows a note of doubt to creep
in as to whether the Disciples' experience had been a
perception of reality. They ask

> Was it a vision?*
> Or did we see that day the unseeable
> One glory of the everlasting world . . . ?

The question is not answered. Their experience was a fact; beyond that they will not go.

> Reality or vision, this we have seen.

It may seem odd that a poem supposedly spoken by the Disciples should not express a robuster faith, and should not be more specifically Christian. There is no point in complaining of this; one must accept the poem on its own terms. All Muir's best religious poems are expressions of what he had felt, seen, or imagined. He was very chary of erecting a structure of belief on his experiences, though he admitted to faith in immortality, and later in the Incarnation. Even with regard to immortality he was anxious to evade the question of belief: "Immortality is not an idea or a belief, but a state of being in which man keeps alive in himself his perception of that boundless union and freedom, which he can faintly apprehend in time, though its consummation lies beyond time."[14] There is some confusion of thought here, since to speak of a consummation beyond time is to express a belief, whether he likes it or not.

In these late poems Muir is not so much meditating on different ideas about human destiny as exploring different states of being. One is symbolised by the Labyrinth (being enclosed within the self); the other is seen in "The Transfiguration" (a going out from the self which produces a sense of freedom and union). These states have relevance not only to each man's personal life, but to social life as well. The one state of being produces strife, wars, and ultimately may lead to the total destruction of man in an atomic war. The other could produce, in Muir's terms, a remaking of our City, the establishment of an ordered and free common-

* An early version read: "Was it delusion?"

wealth. Much of the rest of his work was to be an exploration of these two contrary states of the human soul and of their consequences.

A state of conflict is notoriously easier to convey imaginatively than one of peace, and "The Transfiguration," though beautiful and moving, is perhaps less completely satisfying as a poem than "The Combat," Muir's finest poem based on a dream. A prose account of the dream is given in the *Autobiography*.[15] In the dream he saw the two creatures, just as they are described in the poem—the fierce splendidly-coloured one and the earth-coloured one with soft, brown eyes. As the two stood ready to fight he could see from their look that they "knew each other, that they had fought a countless number of times and after this battle would fight again, that each meeting would be the first meeting and that the dark, patient animal would always be defeated, and the bright, fierce animal would always win. I did not see the fight, but I knew it would be ruthless and shameful, with a meaning perhaps, but no comfort." The poem extends the dream by showing the fight, in which the brown-eyed creature is defeated, but escapes death and, after a pause, returns to fight again. Rightly there is no attempt to explain the meaning of the combat or of the two animals. But the poem is, though mysterious, not at all vague. We are made to see the fight, and to share the emotions of the spectator, and even of the combatants. The imaginative effect is all the greater for the fact that whatever meaning there may be in the fight is wholly embodied in the description of it.

The dream seemed to Muir to have "meaning perhaps, but no comfort." Possibly it arose out of his preoccupation as a young man with the idea of perpetual recurrence. No end to the series of combats is in sight. The brown-eyed animal is to return again and again to suffer pain and humiliation; the killing beast is to strike

again and again, but never to succeed in destroying his
enemy. They are in a labyrinth from which there is
apparently no escape. Time, and the conflicts that take
place in it, seem to be all; the only eternity is recurrence.
Nevertheless one might think that there is some comfort
in the fact that the brown-eyed animal is never finally
defeated, and in the other animal's near-despair at the
end. By the time of writing the poem (probably not long
before its publication in 1947, and long after he had had
the dream) Nietzsche was no longer important to Muir,
and he had seen more of the power of evil in the actual
world—of the power of evil, and also of the quiet persistence of good. These later experiences are combined
with the material originally provided by the dream.
That there is hope in the poem, as he himself finally
understood it, is confirmed by his own comment at the
end of a tape-recording of it made at Harvard in 1955:

> Helpless . . . little animal . . . might be a . . . or stand
> for something in humanity that can be killed—that,
> that cannot be killed, actually—that is always at-
> tacked, that is in a very vulnerable position. It is very
> valuable . . . that after it has . . . been . . . beaten or
> vanquished, it does return again. It's in a way, it's
> a . . . rather horrible [way?] but it's an expression of
> hope at the same time, at the end. I take it to be
> something like that. Or it might be taken as humanity
> and all the enormous forces, particularly nowadays,
> ranged against humanity in every way.*

He was evidently speaking impromptu, fumbling for
words. With characteristic modesty he did not claim to
be able to give an authoritative interpretation of his own
poem, which had taken shape in his imagination at a
deeper level than that of conscious thought. But what he
says confirms one's feeling that the poem makes a dual,
though not a confused, impression. It expresses both the

* Here the dots represent hesitations in speech, not omissions.

horror and the hope with which a man of sensitivity and faith may contemplate the modern world.

In choosing the above three poems from *The Labyrinth* to comment on, I have emphasised perhaps too much Muir's use of myth and dream. For he often writes more directly of normal and present-day experience, though when he does so it is usually that something he has seen or felt in the present has enabled him to write with new precision on an old theme. An example is "The Good Town."[16] He had for long brooded on the theme of betrayal. At the beginning of the novel, *The Three Brothers*, the boy David Blackadder is greatly upset when his father comes back from St Andrews with the news that "the Cardinal [Beaton] has been killed in the Castle." He learns that the killers got into the supposedly impregnable place by a little secret gate. The thought that "a man can be killed in the middle of a castle" strikes the boy's imagination powerfully. The idea of treachery was added to that of the stealthly penetration of a place thought secure in the poem "The Castle."[17] The defenders lay at ease believing themselves safe, but

> There was a little private gate
> A little wicked wicket gate.
> The wizened warder let them through.
>
> Oh then our maze of tunnelled stone
> Grew thin and treacherous as air.

Their enemy was gold, which corrupted the warder; and against that they could not fight. And there are more subtle means of corruption than gold. In an earlier poem refugees meditate:

> A crack ran through our hearthstone long ago,
> And from the fissure we watched gently grow
> The tame domesticated danger,
> Yet lived in comfort in our haunted rooms.[18]

They had watched others homeless, and had not cared

enough, and are now homeless themselves. Wrong had come upon them from outside, but the evil had been in themselves too, and had made them vulnerable. The strong place may fall also because of division between classes. In an early poem a Trojan, now a slave of the Greeks, remembers how Troy fell because the leaders would not trust the common people with arms

> And while they feared the Greeks they feared us most,
> And ancient Troy was lost and we were lost.[19]

The destruction of a good order from without and at the same time its betrayal from within—before 1948 this had been something Muir had read about in history, thought about, and contemplated from afar. In 1948 in Prague he saw it happening before his eyes. The good town is both Prague and any good order destroyed in a similar way. The poem is spoken by the old citizens who had known the days before the two great wars, when there had been

> streets of friendly neighbours,
> Street friend to street and house to house. In summer
> All day the doors stood open; ...

Now a series of calamities have brought not only physical destruction to the town, but also inner corruption:

> And now you see our town, the fine new prison,
> The house-doors shut and barred, the frightened faces
> Peeping round corners, secret police, informers,
> And all afraid of all.

How did it happen? It seemed to come from the outside, but sometimes the old citizens ask themselves

> 'Could it have come from us? Was our peace peace?
> Our goodness goodness? That old life was easy
> And kind and comfortable; but evil is restless
> And gives no rest to the cruel or the kind.'

Even within the good order evil was present; the very sense of security was itself a danger—as it had been to

Cardinal Beaton and to the defenders in "The Castle."
So "The Good Town" is not only about the fall of
Prague to the Communists, though it is given strength
and immediacy by Muir's experience of that event; it is
about the Fall, as a result of which the restless evil is ever
present. Muir's later poems show, along with an increasing confidence in the possibility of rediscovering
Eden, an increasingly realistic and impassioned awareness of the pervasiveness of evil.

The poems in *The Labyrinth* are of a more consistently
high standard than in any previous volume. The writing
has a luminous simplicity. Image and theme are more
perfectly united, and the range and complexity of
reference of the symbols is greater. Where was he to go
from there? He had found his way out of the Labyrinth,
had attained to a vision of wholeness and peace, had
gone back over his past and tried to sum up what he had
learned from it. What more was there to say? The next
volume, *One Foot in Eden* (1956), breaks new ground in
two ways. First, the poems in the first section are ar-
ranged in a sequence and together present a more com-
prehensive vision of the whole of human history than he
had attempted before. They deal in turn with the creation, Eden and the Fall, Greek myths, Abraham, the
Annunciation, Incarnation, and Passion, and with man's
present condition. An introductory poem, "Milton"
celebrates an earlier poet who also had written of the
cycle of Paradise lost and regained; a final one, "The
Emblem," treats of the imaginative world which Muir
himself has created in his poetry. I do not suppose these
poems were written with any idea of forming a whole,
but in a rough way they do; and they gain in richness of
meaning by being read together. Muir has now come to
understand more clearly the meanings of his dreams and
intuitions, and to be able to arrange them in a whole.
Secondly, *One Foot in Eden* explores new territory by incorporating, though not with consistent success, Muir's

fuller realisation of the Incarnation, which his time in Italy had given him. If this volume is not so consistently good as its predecessor, it is for an honourable reason. The old man was still a voyager.

Professor Holloway has commented[20] penetratingly on three of the earlier poems in the first part of *One Foot in Eden*—"Milton," "Orpheus' Dream," and "Telemachos Remembers," showing the superiority of the last of these, in concreteness and in range and complexity of meaning, to the earlier treatment of the Penelope story in "The Return of Odysseus." So I shall confine myself here to the final twelve poems in the series, which are the ones which explore most new territory.

Of the six poems which deal with the central events of the Christian story, Muir excluded four from the final collection. These are the ones which are most orthodoxly Christian. I do not know whether these exclusions mean as Mr Hamburger thinks,[21] that Muir "was anxious to remain uncommitted to the last"; or merely that he realised the inferiority of the poems to his best work. The only one of the six which is among his best is "The Annunciation," which grew directly out of an experience in Italy, recorded in the *Autobiography*:

> I remember stopping for a long time one day to look at a small plaque on the wall of a house in the Via degli Artisti, representing the Annunciation. An angel and a young girl, their bodies inclined towards each other, their knees bent as if overcome by love, 'tutto tremante', gazed upon each other like Dante's pair; and that representation of a human love so intense that it could not reach farther seemed the perfect earthly symbol of the love which passes understanding.[22]

The Annunciation was thus made real to his imagination, and he conveys his excitement in the resulting poem, which has a wonderful glow and intensity. In writing of the Nativity and of the Passion he was attempting themes

which were as yet beyond him because they had not,
apparently, been to the same extent made real to him by
experience.

After glancing at some key points, he looks back in the
title poem[23] and sums up what has gone before. This
poem presents his mature vision both of his own life and
of human history. "The world's great day is growing
late," and his own life is drawing near its end. Looking
back over the fields of time he sees both the good and the
evil, the love and the hate which he has known in his life,
and these things as they have perpetually existed together throughout history. The personal memories
("famished field and blackened tree" and "these
beclouded skies" make us think of his time in Glasgow,
and, by implication, of his earlier personal Eden) are
contained within the larger vision of human history, in
which hope and faith and pity and love have blossomed
in a way that they would not have in a state of sinlessness
without struggle. The familiar large theme is given new
life by being embodied in well-chosen images.

> Yet still from Eden springs the root
> As clean as on the starting day

and the following lines do much more than make a statement about the persistence through time of something of
the unfallen world. The perpetually renewed beauty of
nature is not presented simply as a symbol pointing to
something beyond itself; in a sense it is Eden, existing
now and always.

Distinctive of Muir is the adjective "armorial" in the
lines:

> And nothing now can separate
> The corn and tares compactly grown.
> The armorial weed in stillness bound
> About the stalk....

He was fond of using images from heraldry. The word

G

"armorial" makes us see the weed bound round the stalk as a heraldic device, a static pattern abstracted from the processes of time. This is appropriate here. The poem makes us look, not at the changes happening within time (the particular weed growing up round the stalk and then dying), but at the things that are happening always —or, at least, recurrently. We contemplate as in an eternal present the root springing clean from the earth, the withered leaves, the corn and the tares standing together. The words "armorial" applied to weed and "archetypal" applied to leaf do more here than more visually descriptive adjectives would have done. "Armorial" draws one's attention to the possible heraldic meanings of other words in the poem. "Field" can be used as a heraldic term, for the background upon which an emblem is painted. So perhaps the weed bound round the corn can be taken as the emblem of humanity painted on the blackened "field" of time. Also "from Eden springs the root" suggests a tree, and this could be both a natural tree and the family tree of humanity springing from Adam. Both nature and man take their origin from Eden.

Even though "the broken Eden" still exists, both within people and in the natural world, and even though the Incarnation may have pointed the way by which it may be made whole again, that is not the end of the story. The Incarnate One can be betrayed, and anything good that has been built up can be allowed to decay. This is the theme of the next three poems. The Incarnation is dealt with most effectively in this volume not directly, but in a poem about its betrayal, "The Incarnate One."[24] This poem, like some others we have considered, gathers up ideas from earlier writings, combining them with something new and so incorporating them in a wider context. Muir had written often of the material exploitation of Scotland, of its political and other divisions, and of its spiritual and cultural impoverishment; these last he connected with Puritanism, and, more specifically, with Calvinism:

> We were a tribe, a family, a people . . .
> But Knox and Melville clapped their preaching palms
> And bundled all the harvesters away,
> Hoodicrow Peden in the blighted corn
> Hacked with his rusty beak the starving haulms.[25]

In a prose essay already mentioned he had pointed out what he considered the likenesses between Calvinism and Marxism—both, to his mind, inhuman, impersonal systems. In recent years he had become increasingly concerned about the de-personalising effects of modern systems—industrial, political, and ideological. Now he sees all these things as denials of the Incarnation. In Christ the antinomy of flesh and spirit, time and eternity is resolved. The Word became flesh, Christ walked the earth as a person. The infinite value of each person and the rightness of expressing divine mysteries through images are among the implications of this. Calvinism turned mystery into system, and re-introduced division:

> The windless northern surge, the sea-gull's scream,
> And Calvin's kirk crowning the barren brae.
> I think of Giotto the Tuscan shepherd's dream,
> Christ, man and creature in their inner day.
> How could our race betray
> The Image, and the Incarnate one unmake
> Who chose this form and fashion for our sake?
>
> The Word made flesh here is made word again,
> A word made word in flourish and arrogant crook. . . .

Calvinism was the "fleshless word" that brought spiritual impoverishment to Scotland in the past; to-day we are in danger from a new tyranny of the same kind, the new fleshless word of those who seek to "build their cold empire on the abstract man."

This fine poem is followed by two others, "Scotland's Winter" and "The Great House," which deal in a slighter way with the themes of betrayal and decay. The first of these was first published much earlier in *Scottish Journey*, and was the crystallisation of Muir's "impressions of Edinburgh, or rather of historical Scotland, [his] feeling of the contrast between its legendary past and its tawdry present."[26] It gains by being included in its new context. Taken by itself it expresses no more than what may seem rather a sentimental nostalgia. The heels of the modern girl as she goes by seem to be mocking the great dead who lie below; she cares nothing for the legendary past of Scotland, and is content with the shallow present. Since writing that poem Muir had come to understand more clearly, he believed, the nature of, and the reason for, Scotland's winter. We can connect the "poor frozen life" and the ice which "lays its smooth claws on the sill" in the earlier poem with the more richly significant images of cold in "The Incarnate One."

The final poem in the series is "The Emblem":

> I who so carefully keep in such repair
> The six-inch king and the toy treasury,
> Prince, poet, realm shrivelled in time's black air,
> I am not, although I seem, an antiquary.
> For that scant-acre kingdom is not dead,
> Nor save in seeming shrunk. When at its gate,
> Which you pass daily, you incline your head,
> And enter (do not knock; it keeps no state)
>
> You will be with space and order magistral,
> And that contracted world so vast will grow
> That this will seem a little tangled field.
> For you will be in very truth with all
> In their due place and honour, row on row.
> For this I read the emblem on the shield.[27]

In connexion with this poem it is of interest to read Muir's article on "Toys and Abstractions" in *The Saltire*

Review.[28] Toys, he wrote, are "the first works of art in our experience, and should help us to recapture the feelings of the first artist and the first spectator." The poem is primarily about the artist, specifically Muir himself, in the act of creation, who makes a world where all things are ordered. The world of images which the artist creates may at first seem a trivial toy world remote from ordinary experience and from the present ("I seem, an antiquary"); but it is in fact neither small nor dead nor remote. The realm of imaginative vision is not far off ("You pass daily"); anyone who enters it will find that it is "this" (the ordinary every-day world un-illuminated by the imagination) that is, in comparison, but "a little tangled field." In a quieter, less pretentious way Muir here reasserts the faith of the great romantics in the imagination. In this realm of imaginative vision "you will be *in very truth* with all in their due place and honour." This vision is not mere fantasy, but perception. What distinguishes this poem from the many others that make large claims for the poetic imagination is the quiet-ness of tone and the genuine modesty contained in it. He does not set himself as Bard apart from the common many. "I" and "you" are not opposed; both can attain to vision. The quietness of tone and the plainness of the diction help to convey the meaning, to express the idea that the way of seeing spoken of is not exclusive to a few, not to be attained by difficult, esoteric means. Humility is suggested not only by what is said ("you incline your head") but also by the way it is said. The poem makes a fitting end to the section.

The poems in the second section of *One Foot in Eden* do not fall into any definite sequence like those in the first. They deal more with the specific problems of passing through "the difficult land" of time than with the com-prehensive vision of time in relation to eternity (though this is always in the background). Quite a variety of moods is expressed. In some poems, as in "Effigies," he shows himself capable of sharp as well as compassionate observation of character; in a few others he proves that he did not always need such an object as a shield in order to read an emblem, but that he was also able to use material provided by observation of common things. "The Late Wasp" and "The Late Swallow,"[29] which should be read together, are examples of this second point. They are quite satisfying if taken to express only a delicate sympathy with animal life. The wasp, which used to come each morning to gorge itself on marmalade at the breakfast table, now feels the air grow colder; it can fly no more through "the familiar avenues of the air," and dives down "through nothing and through despair." The swallow has stayed after its comrades, and now must fly south

> Till falling down the homing air
> You light and perch upon the radiant tree.

After reading the poems quite simply one remembers that Muir was nearing seventy and must sometimes have thought of his approaching death. Would death be, for him, just a leaving of familiar things and a descent into nothingness, or would it be a coming home to a more radiant world? The poems are all the more effective for not asking this question openly, and for not answering it at all (unless the order in which they are placed may hint an answer).

The new poems in *Collected Poems* (1960), all written during his last five years, show Muir still exploring the present and the future as well as the past. "The Brothers" spans fifty years into the past, recording a dream which gave back to him the memory of his long-dead brothers, now transfigured so that he can see in them "the beauty and the buried grace" which had been masked in life because they had striven "for victory." His last poem, "I have been taught," fittingly brings his work to a close by expressing his gratitude for all that he had learned from the past—from parents and friends now dead, and from literature. But these last poems are, in general, less concerned with the past and with merely personal problems than those in the two preceding volumes, and more with the condition of the world around him, with the war and its consequences and with the possible disasters to come. A central theme is man's failure to be able to feel these large calamities personally. A single grief can change us, and so

> bring a stern relief.
> A son or a daughter dead
> Can bend the back or whiten the head,
> Break and remould the heart. . . .

But

> The impersonal calamities estrange us
> From our own selves, send us abroad
> In desolate thoughtlessness,
> While far behind our hearts know what they know,
> Yet cannot feel, nor ever express.[30]

This is connected with two poems, "Ballad of Everyman" and "Nightmare of Peace" (versions of the same poem, neither brought to a quite satisfactory state), in which a frightening vision is shown of the consequences of failure to treat individuals as persons.

Among the most impressive of the late poems are those which deal with a possible atomic war. He does not concentrate on the physical horrors, but on what might be the feelings of a sensitive person confronted by universal destruction:

> No place at all for bravery in that war
> Nor mark where one might make a stand,
> No use for eye or hand
> To discover and reach the enemy
> Hidden in boundless air.
> No way to attempt, to save
> By our own death the young. . . .[31]

He goes on to imagine very vividly what might be one's
thoughts and feelings near the end; and then returns to
the present, in which he finds cause for both hope and
fear:

> our help is in all that is full-grown
> In nature and all that is with hands well-made, ...
> There is the harmony
> By which we know our own and the world's health.

We see harmony and creativeness around us in nature
and in the works of men's hands; but perhaps these
things are not enough; for, due to a lack of sufficient
sympathy, we have failed to translate this harmony into
terms of social life:

> We who were wrapped so warm in foolish joys
> Did not have time to call on pity
> For all that is sick, and heal and remake our city.

The thought is taken further in another terrifying poem,
"The Day Before The Last Day."[32] It is man's failure in
imaginative sympathy which prevents him remaking our
city and so forestalling disaster. So on the last day each
man is shown as closed in upon himself, indifferent to
others, in the labyrinth of his own loneliness. All

> Think only of themselves and curse the faithless earth.

As the last day dawns no great vision comes; but all stare
in silence at the sun they shall not see set, and think

> 'Choose! Choose again, you who have chosen this!
> Too late! Too late!'

That end is what they themselves have chosen, and it is
now too late to choose again.

But perhaps there will be some survivors, even of an
atomic war. What will their life be like? Two poems
present, with equal power, visions of two different possibilities. In "After a Hypothetical War"[33] we are shown

a poisoned earth, and a state of anarchy in which each
man grabs for what little food remains:

> No rule nor ruler: only water and clay,
> And the purblind peasant squatting, elbows out
> To nudge his neighbour from his inch of ground. . . .

The city which we failed to remake has been completely
destroyed, and there seems no possibility of renewal.
An earlier poem, "The Horses,"[34] from *One Foot in Eden*,
offers a vision of a more hopeful kind. A renewal of life
comes through a regaining of man's old companionship
with animals. Here again old themes, which had long
been favourites, are combined with a new one. From
early days he had had a special feeling for animals. In
the *Autobiography* he had written of the primitive companionship of men and animals, something of which still
existed in the Orkneys in his childhood; of his mixed
feelings of awe and delight and repulsion aroused by the
animals on his father's farm; of man's feelings of guilt
with respect to the animals which he kills and uses.
Many of his dreams had been about animals, both real
and fabulous; in his dreams of Paradise animals always
had their place; and animals had figured largely in his
poems. In modern industrial life he had found a sense
of alienation—of men from the earth and the animals,
of men from each other. The human community, the
city, is broken, and the at-oneness between the human
community and the natural environment. It was natural
for him to connect these things with the new fear of
atomic war; for such a war could be seen as the final
fruit of man's misuse of nature. In "The Horses" the
situation of a remote community that has escaped destruction in war (a "seven days war"—seven days of destruction corresponding to the Biblical seven days of creation)
is vividly imagined. The radios stand silent in the rooms;
a warship passes, its decks piled with dead; an aeroplane
plunges overhead into the sea. The people return to pre-

industrial conditions, except that the relics of industrialism lie around them; the tractors rust in the fields. Then the horses come, as if under command to find again "that long-lost archaic companionship" with men. Among them are colts, born since the war,

> Dropped in some wilderness of the broken world,
> Yet new as if they had come from their own Eden.

Life is renewing itself in them; one remembers "Still from Eden springs the root as clean. . . ." At first the men look with wonder at the horses, not thinking of them as "creatures to be owned and used"; but they enter into their "free servitude" to men again; their coming was a new beginning.

Any suggestion that this poem is too easily optimistic is contradicted by the later more sombre ones. The poet is not a prophet in the sense of being able to foretell the future. He cannot say that there will or will not be an atomic war, nor that after such a war life will or will not be renewed; and Muir does not try to do so. He is a prophet only in the sense of having an unusually impassioned awareness of the forces working in the present —both of those which make for destruction and division and of those which make for harmony and wholeness. In these poems Muir presents with great imaginative power visions of some of the possible ends these forces might lead to. In them he shows again that he was not, though some have thought him so, "an antiquary." He had been "taught by dreams and fantasies," but had not retreated into them. Taught by them he was able to look at the contemporary world and at the "tangled field" of common experience, and to illuminate them in a way which is not possible for those who know nothing but the fragmentary experiences of the moment.

REFERENCES

1. *C.P.*, p. 114.
2. "Telemachos Remembers," in *C.P.*, pp. 219–20.
3. *C.P.*, pp. 92–3.
4. *C.P.*, pp. 93–4.
5. Letter to Raymond Tschumi, 10 Jun. 1949, quoted in *Thought in Twentieth Century English Poetry.*
6. *C.P.*, p. 105.
7. *C.P.*, pp. 115–16.
8. *C.P.*, p. 48.
9. *C.P.*, pp. 163–5.
10. *C.P.*, p. 199.
11. *C.P.*, pp. 198–200.
12. *A.*, p. 114.
13. *A.*, p. 115.
14. *A.*, p. 170.
15. *A.*, p. 65.
16. *C.P.*, pp. 183–6.
17. *C.P.*, pp. 128–9.
18. "The Refugees," in *C.P.*, pp. 95–6.
19. "The Trojan Slave," in *C.P.*, pp. 72–3.
20. *The Hudson Review*, XIII (1960–1).
21. *Encounter*, Dec. 1960.
22. *A.*, p. 278.
23. *C.P.*, p. 227.
24. *C.P.*, pp. 228–9.
25. "Scotland 1941," in *C.P.*, p. 97.
26. *S.J.*, p. 38.
27. *C.P.*, pp. 230–1.
28. *Saltire Review*, Winter 1957.
29. *C.P.*, p. 253.
30. "Impersonal Calamity," in *C.P.*, pp. 280–1.
31. "The Last War," in *C.P.*, pp. 281–4.
32. *C.P.*, pp. 299–300.
33. *C.P.*, p. 265.
34. *C.P.*, pp. 246–7.

CHAPTER VI

CONCLUSION

Muir's reputation as a poet grew gradually. In the nineteen-twenties and thirties he was known mainly as a critic and translator, and his poetry did not have a very wide sale. Those who knew it well recognised it as the work of a man of great integrity, trying to say something of his own in his own way; but to most readers it was not so exciting as the work of those who were making more startling innovations in technique or who seemed to be dealing in a more direct and challenging way with the contemporary world. His reputation grew in the nineteen-forties with his increasing mastery of his medium, and a second impression of *The Labyrinth* was called for within a year of publication. It was not until the last decade of his life, however, that influential critics began to claim for him a place among the major poets of the century. Mr William Arrowsmith, for instance, reviewing in *The Hudson Review* (Winter 1954) the American edition of his *Collected Poems*, judged it the finest volume of poetry that had appeared for a long time—since the last and best of Yeats or even since Hardy. He found in Muir's "A Birthday" "more genuine mastery of language and experience than in twenty pages of Dylan Thomas." Recently it has been more generally realized that, for all his preoccupation with dreams and myths, his work does illuminate contemporary life as we know it. That he had intelligence, wisdom, vision, is generally acknowledged. To some it seems that in his later poems his vision is conveyed with such beauty and power that he must be regarded as one of the few major poets of our time; others, however, doubt whether his work, however interesting its content, has the strictly poetic qualities that we expect in a major poet.

Criticism of Muir has been mainly in reviews and articles. Mr J. C. Hall in his British Council pamphlet made a good survey of his life and works; in the second chapter of his *Thought in Twentieth Century Poetry* Mr Raymond Tschumi wrote helpfully of the thought in his poetry; among the articles I have found especially valuable Professor Holloway's in *The Hudson Review* (Winter 1960–61). I have listed the most interesting articles I have come across in the bibliography, and will not summarise them here. Making use of what I have learned from them, I will try first to state the point of view of those who do not consider Muir a major poet, then to answer these criticisms, and in so doing to define my own view.

The reservations that have been expressed about Muir's poetry can be summarised under three heads. (1) It is said that his work is lacking in "that linguistic vitality without which true poetry cannot exist."[1] (2) It is said that his verse is not rhythmically exciting; that it has "only occasionally that dionysiac lift . . . that turns good verse into great poetry."[2] (3) It is said that "his imagery is generally beautiful, but dead: that is to say, suppose he introduces a lion, he treats it as if it were a heraldic animal—its mythic or symbolic value ossifying the live brute."[3] This last criticism is sometimes extended to a complaint that his whole created world is too much of an artificial construct, is lacking in flesh and blood reality, does not contain enough of the actualities of the world we know.

Most critics concede that these strictures do not apply to all his poems; but it is sometimes said that his work as a whole is lacking in gaiety, that it is too continuously solemn.

In answer to these more general criticisms one must acknowledge the absence from Muir's poetry of "gaiety"

—though there are touches of humour, as in "There's
Nothing Here." This does not mean, however, that the
total effect of the poetry is a gloomy one. There is joy in
the poems—a much bigger thing than gaiety. There are
moments of ecstatic vision, as in "The Transfiguration,"
and, more characteristically, the expression of a deep,
abiding joy in things that endure—found, for instance,
in the love poems, and in poems expressing his gratitude
to the past and his recovered delight in nature. This quiet
joy, not easily won, comes from a deeper source and is in
the long run much more valuable than an outburst of
gaiety. Muir's poetry is consistently and openly serious.
But obviously this is not a defect. One wants different
kinds of poetry—the light, the humorous, the kind that
is apparently light but has underlying seriousness, and so
on as well as the openly serious; but one does not expect
every poet to give us everything. Similarly, one concedes
that there is little irony in his work. There are different
levels of meaning in many of his poems, but these are not
related to one another in the way they are when irony is
being used. He seldom, if ever, says a thing in such a way
as to suggest that his real meaning is the opposite to that
which appears on the surface. But clearly irony is not a
necessary ingredient in all good poetry. These criticisms
amount to no more than saying that Muir wrote certain
kinds of poetry, and not others.

To return to the more specific complaints—it is difficult to answer the charge of absence of linguistic vigour
except by quoting at great length. A poem has to be
grasped as a whole before one can appreciate the full
force of the particular words in it. This is true of all poets,
of course; but is especially so of Muir. One could demonstrate the linguistic vitality of such a poet as Yeats by
quoting single lines. But, though one can think of some
lines of Muir's which are individually striking—either for
their epigrammatic terseness ("The Word made flesh
here is made word again")[4] or for their cadence and

large simplicity of utterance ("And vast compassion curving like the skies")[5]—he is not in general well represented by short extracts. His diction is not highly-coloured. Simple, ordinary, and even prosaic-sounding words can come to have great force when rightly placed in a whole that gives them significance. The special effect which his poems make is partly due to their quietness of tone, to the absence of showing-off. He is wholly absorbed in what he wants to say. It is in the tactful placing of words rather than by the choice of individually striking ones that he shows his art. Striking words may draw attention to themselves, and so spoil the total effect.

To substantiate this it would be necessary to quote and analyse at length whole poems. If one considers carefully almost any of the shorter poems from Muir's mature work one finds that each word is right and meaningful in its context, though few lines and phrases would sound very exciting if detached. In "In Love for Long"[6] the simple words "sweet" and "wild" have great force when paradoxically combined with "imprisonment" in

> And in imprisonment
> Flourishes sweet and wild . . .;

and the rather prosaic-sounding word "established" is just what is needed in

> A breath, yet as still
> As the established hill.

Or take the last two sections of "The Annunciation"[7]

> Outside the window footsteps fall
> Into the ordinary day
> And with the sun along the wall
> Pursue their unreturning way.
>
> Sound's perpetual roundabout
> Rolls its numbered octaves out
> And hoarsely grinds its battered tune.

> But through the endless afternoon
> These neither speak nor motion make,
> But stare into their deepening trance
> As if their gaze would never break.

In the second line quoted no more spectacular word would be so effective, both in cadence and meaning, as "ordinary." The contrast between the everyday world and the deepening trance in which angel and girl are met is well suggested in the harsh line

> And hoarsely grinds its battered tune.

followed by the quiet, smooth-flowing final lines. The contrast, however, is not too great. A lesser poet might have been tempted to let the external world break in more violently in order to show off his ability to handle different metrical effects. The trance would then have been broken—or at any rate the reader's attention would have been distracted from it. This is not what is needed here. The poet needs to show a consciousness of the ordinary world going on, but to let it be heard only mutedly. This is what he achieves. The break in the prevailing quietness of tone at the end of the penultimate section is just sufficient without being too great. The effect created here, as in many of the late poems, is one of quiet wonder. Violent contrasts in diction or imagery or rhythm would not be in place.

Perhaps the most distinctive thing about Muir's diction is his ability to use the great commonplace words, such as "good, true, beauty, love, peace," without opening himself to the charge of vagueness or of inflation. "The Confirmation,"[8] for instance is full of such elemental words ("love, false, true, honest and good, beautiful") and of simple elemental images ("twisting roads, a fountain in a waste, the blowing seed, the hearth"); yet the poem makes a quite distinct and very powerful impression; and breathes an air of complete sincerity. Few, especially modern, poets dare to write so straightforwardly without "cleverness" or irony. But to speak of daring is wrong. Muir is not consciously defying the fashion, but is simply seeking, and finding, the right words to convey his experiences.

Muir is sometimes contrasted to his disadvantage with Yeats; but both use words in ways which are appropriate to what they have to convey. Yeats makes his old pensioner say

> I spit into the face of Time
> That has transfigured me.

Here the colloquial violence of "spit" contrasted with the noble associations of "transfigured" makes a very powerful effect. Yeats is deliberately theatrical; he strikes extreme attitudes, bringing contrary emotions into collision. Here the old pensioner at the same time rails bitterly against time and expresses a sense of triumph over it. The word "transfigured" can be understood both ironically and straightforwardly. Muir does not achieve this sort of effect, and he does not aim to. There is nothing of the theatrical about him; he does not wear any masks. To express the extreme contrasts of emotions which his poems contain Yeats's combination of coarsely colloquial and noble diction was appropriate. Muir's quieter and less varied diction was also appropriate to his purposes. When Yeats wanted to express a quiet wonder, as in "Ribh at the Tomb of Baile and Ailinn," he, too, uses simple and unspectacular words. His lovers "hurry into each other's arms"; this is right in the same way as the diction of "The Annunciation" is right. His old pensioner's diction is right in a way which would not be so for Muir. There is a greater range and variety in the work of Yeats; on the other hand, there is in the mature work of Muir a greater sense of wholeness, of tensions having been resolved. Truth may obey the call not only of those who batter on the wall.

H

I would answer the charge of lack of rhythmical excitement in much the same way. One acknowledges that some poets use a wider variety of rhythmical effects and appeal more powerfully to the senses than Muir does; but within his chosen field he achieves what he aims at. His is reflective poetry, not usually recreating the variations of feeling from moment to moment, but pondering on experiences which have been mastered and understood. He writes of the Labyrinth after he has come out from it. The emotion is recollected in tranquillity. For this kind of poetry Muir, like Wordsworth, found rather slow and grave and unobtrusive rhythms appropriate. "The gods approve the depth, and not the tumult of the soul." The tumults are there, but contained within a framework of calm. We have seen how this situation is reflected in the changes, not too great, of rhythm in "The Annunciation." A less subtle example is the sonnet, "Comfort in Self-Despite."[9] The tumult of feeling in the opening lines is reflected in unusually emphatic alliteration:

> When in revulsion I detest myself
> Thus heartily, myself with myself appal,
> And in this mortal rubbish delve and delve,
> A dustman damned—

and is then stilled by the thought of how, after speaking ill of a friend,

> Remembrance clears his image and I see
> The pure and touching good no taunt could kill.

The formality of the sonnet helps to give the effect of containing the agitation within a structure in which it is overcome.

Muir's quiet manner should not make us fail to recognise his mastery of difficult metrical forms. The apparent ease and the lucidity of his best writing were attained by much hard work, as the state of his notebooks shows. In particular he was a master of the sonnet, of which he wrote eighteen in his mature years. I cannot think of any other modern poet who can match these eighteen sonnets. They are all well-constructed, and give a sense of neatness and completeness, reminiscent of the work of George Herbert. In "Comfort in Self-Despite" and in "The Transmutation" the octet and the sestet are each made up of single sentences, which run quite naturally in the metrical pattern. The unobtrusive skill with which long sentences are fitted into metre is seen also in other forms. "The Day" consists of one perfectly lucid sentence of seventeen lines; "Reading in Wartime" consists again of a single sentence, this time of thirty-nine-three-stressed lines, rhyming irregularly; the first thirty-four and a half lines of "The Labyrinth" are made up of a single sentence, as are the first twenty-four lines of the seventh section of "The Journey Back." These feats were not achieved in order to show off, but because they were relevant to his purposes. His poems frequently develop a closely-knit argument; and the bringing-together of a number of thoughts and images into a single sentence helps to show their connexion. The sentence referred to in "The Journey Back" mirrors in its structure the thought by winding through its long course to an end which gives a sense of finality, of rest, of coming home:

> And the tumultuous world slips softly home
> To its perpetual end and flawless bourne.[10]

In Muir sound serves sense unobtrusively. Means are subordinated to ends. One is not at first captivated by the sound for its own sake; but after one has experienced a poem as a whole one can look back and find that the metre and the variations of rhythm have played their part in helping one to do so. His poems go over very well when read aloud. The lines glow when charged with strong thought and feeling, as they usually are. But, in the longer poems especially, there are inevitably some parts less highly charged than others; and in such passages the musical qualities of the lines are not by themselves enough to sustain interest. "The Difficult Land"[11] is, perhaps, an example of a poem which rises only intermittently to the intensity of poetic utterance. The lines

> We have strange dreams: as that, in the early morning
> We stand and watch the silver drift of stars
> Turn suddenly to a flock of black-birds flying.

are of interest because of the odd and puzzling image. But the fairly commonplace content of the lines that follow is not given any new life by distinction of imagery or rhythm:

> And once in a lifetime men from over the border,
> In early summer, the season of fresh campaigns,
> Come trampling down the corn, and kill our cattle.
> These things we know and by good luck or guidance
> Either frustrate or, if we must, endure. . . .

We return to poetry in the arresting image:

> Enter our darkness through the doors of wheat.

The lines between the two striking images are not especially exciting, but they maintain a respectable standard in view of the fact that they have been especially chosen to demonstrate Muir at his least good. This is the base below which he never, in his mature work, falls. The writing is austere, competent and uninflated. One does not expect all parts of a poem of some length to be equally intense. There are not many successive lines in the mature poems which fail to rise above this not low base. It is in the larger blank verse poems that such rather flat passages most often occur. He hardly ever fails in octosyllabics or in the shorter poems in stanzas, but shows that he has an excellent ear for simple, haunting tunes.

Imagery, like diction and rhythm, must be appreciated

in its context. Clearly there is no reason why a poet should not use images from heraldry, when they are appropriate to his purpose, as I have suggested they are in "One Foot in Eden"; nor why he should not use new fabulous animals of his own creation, provided he can make them real for us in his poem. On the other hand one might well regard it as a limitation if a poet used nothing but such images drawn from literature and myths and dreams rather than from direct observation of the actual world.

Muir was not lacking in sensuous awareness of things, though he does not go in for descriptive writing for its own sake. He mentions in passing

> The tingling smell and touch
> Of dogrose and sweet briar

but goes on, not to describe in more detail the particular things which excited him, but rather to examine the significance of the experience for him. He can describe an actual scene at some length and vividly, as in "The Wayside Station," but more usually finds it enough to sketch it in a few strokes, as in "The Incarnate One":

> The windless northern surge, the sea-gull's scream,
> And Calvin's kirk crowning the barren brae....

He brings in enough descriptive detail for his purpose. One thinks of "the white smoke curling from the silver gun" of the little General; of the spider's web stretched from the enchanted knight's breastplate to his iron hand; of the murderers "with rags tied round their feet for silence"; of the

> gate, a mass of blackened stone
> Crowned with vermilion fiends like streamers blown
> From a great funnel filled with roaring flame

in "Milton"; of the angel's wonder making "each feather tremble on his wings" in "The Annunciation"; and of

many other lines of the same kind. There are actual animals in his poems as well as heraldic and fabulous ones—
horses in several poems, birds in "The Late Swallow"
and "The Bird," the wasp in "The Late Wasp," etc. He
can conjure up the feeling and atmosphere of a scene,
even when he does not describe it in much detail, as in
"Suburban Dream" and "The Interrogation." Sunset
scenes are evoked in "Double Absence" and "Sunset."
There is more detail in the first of these, *e.g.*:

> Now the moon rises clear and fever pale
> Out from the cloud's dissolving drift of ashes

but the second conveys equally well the feeling intended.
The line "The bright cloud showering peace" conveys
more in its context than an exact description of the
colours of the sunset would have done.

More characteristic of him than his descriptions of
actual scenes, however, is his ability to make real some
imagined landscape or incident from mythology or
dream. One remembers Hector seeing with the strange
clarity of dream

> The grasses puff a little dust
> Where my footsteps fall . . .

the enchanted knight, Odysseus' house, the two animals
in "The Combat," the brightness pouring from the heads
of "The Brothers," the nightmare scene before the end of
the world in "The Day before the Last Day." Such poems
speak to the senses and the imagination before they are
understood. In them the poet does not just tell us about
his vision, but enables us to share it. We can then apply
it in various ways to the illumination of daily experience.
In some of the early and in most of the later poems of this
kind the imagined scene or incident is made real and
distinct so as to embody meaning in an unique way. In
some, especially of the early poems, there is a failure
either in the vitality or the suggestiveness of the images.

When we read of travelling along twisting roads and being cut off by mountains from futurity's high-walled land, we may feel that we are just being told something rather obvious about time without the thought being given much freshness. On the other hand, in "Ballad of the Soul," we are not given enough guidance as to how to respond to the scenes described. The failure here is not due to any lack of concreteness, of visualised detail. Indeed there is much more detailed description of things seen than in some of the more successful poems based on dreams; the trouble is failure to give significance to what is described. The same could be said of some others of the early poems—for instance, of parts of *Variations on a Time Theme*. A reader looking only for concreteness might praise

> Splintered stumps, flapping bark, ringwormed boles,
> Soft milk-white water prisoned in jagged holes
> Like gaps where tusks have been. . . .[12]

but not much is made of these details. The much less visually descriptive lines about the root springing clean from Eden in "One Foot in Eden" are far more effective. A few simple and significant images may be more useful than a mass of detail. At his best Muir does not describe anything except when it has significance in relation to the theme of a poem as a whole. A detail that is without significance is an irrelevance. His best poems have an austerity, a simplicity and unity, because of this casting-out of all that is not relevant.

The people who journey through Muir's simply but sufficiently sketched landscapes are not usually sharply individualised.

> The wise king dowered with blessings on his throne,
> The rebel raising his flag in the market place,[13]

are not particularised. The Man and the Woman in "The Sufficient Place" are archetypal figures, "simple and clear as a child's first images." The people, like the landscapes, are endowed with a few simple characteristics; we do not get to know them as complex individuals. Or they are treated collectively; we read of refugees and of "we, the old citizens" of Prague rather than of particular refugees and citizens. Is this at odds with Muir's insistence on the importance of the personal? "The generations tell their personal tale," he wrote; and he justified his wartime reading of Boswell and Tolstoy by the thought that Johnson and Tolstoy's characters taught him more about life, being personal, than figures of war's carnage. A single grief can change us, but the heart cannot respond to large impersonal calamities. He was far removed from those who can "build their cold empire on the abstract man." So it would be strange if his own work were to be found to tend towards the abstract rather than the personal. One must distinguish here between the coldly impersonal and that which is more than merely personal. The line "simple and clear as a child's first images" guides us to what in some of the poems Muir was trying to do. It reminds us of the passage in the *Autobiography* in which he wrote of our first childhood as being the one time in which we live in immortality, when we think of our father and mother, sisters and brothers, as existing in a "vast, boundless calm," in a timeless yet perfectly solid world. This way of seeing is not impersonal nor cold, as the system-maker's way of looking at people as units in a mass is impersonal. "The Sufficient Place" is an attempt to get back to this childhood vision, and therefore rightly excludes the complexities of adult consciousness. Similarly in "The Brothers" he is concerned not to paint portraits of his brothers as they were in every-day life, but to express his recovered sense of the beauty and the buried grace in them which a dream had restored to him. One is reminded, too, of the new way of seeing which followed his first May Day parade in Glasgow, his feeling that all distinctions between people had fallen away and that all substance had been transmuted:

For the first time in my life I began to like ordinary
vulgar people, because in my eyes they were no longer
ordinary or vulgar, since I saw in them shoots of the
glory which they would possess when all men and
women were free and equal. In spite of its simplicity,
this was a genuine imaginative vision of life.[14]

(Later he would have expressed this vision more in
religious than in political terms.) This imaginative vision
sees below the surface distinctions between people; it is
not, in any bad sense, impersonal, but goes beyond, or
deeper than, the merely personal. When we look at the
people in Muir's poems it is sometimes in this way; but
more often we are invited not to look *at* them at all, but
rather through them to make a voyage of discovery into
the possibilities of human experience. It is not what they
are in themselves as distinct individuals that is important,
but what they see and discover. The psychological
"place" that each occupies is usually made clear and
distinct, and what each discovers is usually made real in
precise images.

Muir himself in his poems is a voyager, telling of what
he has discovered rather than of himself or of particular
incidents. In his love-poems, for instance, he does not
describe any particular incidents in his life, nor try to
bring before us very sharply an impression of his wife's
appearance nor even in a precise way of her character.
But the effect the poems make is not at all vague. They
convey with unusual power a feeling of what the experience of lasting love is like, and relate that experience
to others. He is concerned, not with particular moments,
but with what has been built in time's despite over a long
period, and with the meaning of that experience. Fragments of personal experience can find their place in his
poetry only when they have ceased to be mere fragments
and to be merely personal. That this is not due to any
lack of ability to observe particular scenes sharply and to

involve himself in human relationships can be con-
clusively proved from the *Autobiography*—and indeed
from the poems themselves. One can imagine no one less
detached from life than the man who was so filled with
dejection and horror by what he saw in the Glasgow
slums, by the deaths of his brothers, by the plight of
refugees, and the fall of Prague. The *Autobiography* is full
of scenes and incidents from actual life, sharply observed
and described in such a way as to make them deeply
moving. There are some such scenes in the poems, but
not so many as in the *Autobiography*. In telling the story
of his life he could describe scenes and incidents just
because they had struck him; but in writing poetry he
had to wait until such particulars revealed their meaning
and could be appropriately included in the whole which
is a poem.

His world of dreams and myths was as real for him as
the world of every day—indeed in a sense more so.
Dreams and fantasies are "shadows cast by the true."
The every-day world unilluminated by the imagination
is but "a little tangled field" in comparison with the
world entered by the imagination where all are "in their
due place and honour." To enter that world is not to
escape from reality, but to perceive that reality which
gives significance to events which would otherwise be
mere fragments.

Like other modern poets who have tried to see beneath
the surface of life, he was confronted by the special difficulty that there was no agreed system of beliefs, common
to himself and his readers. Earlier poets could attach
their special intuitions to an agreed system of beliefs and
to traditional symbols, thus giving objectivity and univer-
sality to their intuitions and new life to the old beliefs and
symbols. The modern poet may feel that his imaginative
world is a private and personal one, which there is not
much hope of getting others to share; or, if he is anxious
to communicate, he may be tempted to explain and

argue too much. Some of Muir's poems can be criticised along these lines, either for failure to make a private experience into a poem, to make the reader feel the significance of a private symbol, or for making the meaning clear in too obvious a way. But usually he does succeed in conveying his vision either by establishing the significance of personal myths and symbols in the poems or, more often, by attaching personal intuitions to traditional myths, incidents from history, etc. The use of myth came naturally to him, and was never a kind of sophisticated literary game, as it seems to be in some writers. The early poem "Ballad of Hector in Hades" came to him quite spontaneously, and he wrote it down almost complete at a single sitting. He came, spontaneously not by conscious effort, to see the bare landscape of his childhood home as a universal landscape over which the heroes of mythology passed. He always makes the myths he uses very much his own, and gives them a fresh significance. He does not rely on stock responses, nor expect the reader to bring much extraneous knowledge to the understanding of his poems. He sometimes gives rather an unexpected twist to a well-known story, and one must be careful to see exactly what he shows one and not what one might assume one is going to see. For instance, the Orpheus and Eurydice story is treated in quite an original way in "Orpheus' Dream." As Professor Holloway has pointed out, this poem makes use of Greek myth, of neo-Platonic ideas about pre-existence, of traditional images; but it "speaks not *of* these, but *through* them, of the potentialities of our own experience—of what fulfilment in lasting love is like, of how it can come, of what it can yield."[15] In myth and history he sought not an escape from the present, but a means of understanding the present more deeply.

Muir's means were suitable to his ends, to conveying his distinctive vision. As Professor Holloway puts it:

The great central fact about Muir's work is that although in his vision the powers of evil were great, ultimately the powers of good and goodness were greater; and they were greater because they were also humbler, more primaeval, nearer to life in its archaic simplicity; which Muir was able to see not far below life's surface distractions. This, in the end, is the inner vision of joy which the iconic quality of his verse predominantly serves; and it is this sense of the simple but spacious powers of goodness held by life in reserve, that is ultimately what demands, and what justifies, Muir's simple but often monumental imagery; and his grave and lucid rhythms; and the honesty and spareness of his diction.[16]

This "inner vision of joy," the recovered sense of wholeness which some of the late poems convey, is so impressive partly because the more sombre poems show that it had not been won easily. He had been through periods of doubt, of loneliness and near-breakdown; had experienced industrial life at its worst and from the inside, and seen the effects of poverty, disease, unemployment and tyranny in the lives of people close to him; and had shared to the full the fears of thoughtful people in connexion with the atomic bomb. The nighmares characteristic of our century are all present in his poems, as well as the rarer vision of "that boundless union and freedom which [man] can apprehend faintly in time, though its consummation is beyond time." He spoke with complete honesty out of his bewilderment as out of his faith, and though making something whole and well made in his song did not do violence to the mystery of life by claiming to be able to contain it in any neat formula. The best summing-up is in the words of his own last poem on his poetry:

> And in bewilderment
> My tongue shall tell
> What mind had never meant
> Nor memory stored.

In such bewilderment
Love's parable
Into the world was sent
To stammer its word.

What I shall never know
I must make known.
Where traveller never went.
Is my domain.
Dear disembodiment
Through which is shown
The shapes that come and go
And turn again.

Heaven-sent perplexity—
If thought should thieve
One word of the mystery
All would be wrong.
Most faithful fantasy
That can believe
Its immortality
And make a song.[17]

I have enjoyed Muir's poems more than any other new ones I have come across in the last ten years or so. I am confident that he is a genuine poet because he speaks always with an individual voice. I am confident, too, that he is a poet of major importance because of the depth and comprehensiveness of the vision which his poems collectively contain. In comparison the work of most other modern poets seems to me fragmentary. The last time I saw him he told me he was planning a long poem. He did not live to write it, but, in a sense, he had already written it; for his poems, taken together, make up a whole.

REFERENCES

1. Charles Tomlinson in *Pelican Guide to English Literature*, No. 7, p. 469.
2. David Wright in *Encounter*, Jun. 1956, p. 87.
3. *Ibid.*
4. "The Incarnate One," in *C.P.*, p. 228.
5. "The Old Gods," in *C.P.*, p. 120.
6. *C.P.*, p. 159.
7. *C.P.*, p. 224.
8. *C.P.*, p. 118.
9. *C.P.*, p. 154.
10. *C.P.*, p. 175.
11. *C.P.*, pp. 237–8.
12. *C.P.*, p. 39.
13. *C.P.*, p. 116.
14. *A.*, p. 113.
15. *Hudson Review*, XIII (1960–1961), p. 557.
16. *Op. cit.*, pp. 565–6.
17. *C.P.*, p. 285.

BIBLIOGRAPHY

I. EDWIN MUIR

1. Verse

First Poems. London (Hogarth) and New York (Huebsch) 1925.

Chorus of the newly Dead. London (Hogarth) 1926.

Six Poems. Limited edn, Warlingham (Samson Press) 1932. Repr. in *Journeys and Places.*

Variations on a Time Theme. London (Dent) 1934.

Journeys and Places. London (Dent) 1937.

The Narrow Place. London (Faber) 1943.

The Voyage and other Poems. London (Faber) 1946.

The Labyrinth. London (Faber) 1949.

Collected Poems: 1921–1951. Ed. J. C. Hall. London (Faber) 1952; New York (Grove) 1953 and 1957.

Prometheus. Illustrated by John Piper. London (Faber) 1954. Repr. in *One Foot in Eden.*

One Foot in Eden. London (Faber) and New York (Grove) 1956.

Collected Poems: 1921–1958. London (Faber) 1960.

2. Prose

We Moderns. Under the pseudonym "Edward Moore,": London (Allen & Unwin) 1918; New York (Knopf) 1920.

Latitudes. London (Melrose) and New York (Huebsch) 1924.

Transition. London (Hogarth) and New York (Viking) 1926.

The Marionette. London (Hogarth) and New York (Viking) 1927.

Structure of the Novel. London (Hogarth) and New York (Harcourt, Brace) 1928.

John Knox—Portrait of a Calvinist. London (Cape) and New York (Viking) 1929.

The Three Brothers. London (Heinemann) and New York (Doubleday) 1931.

Poor Tom. London (Dent) 1932.

Scottish Journey. London (Heinemann) 1935.

Social Credit and the Labour Party. A pamphlet. London (1935).

Scott and Scotland. London (Routledge) 1936; New York (Speller) 1938.

The Present Age, from 1914. (Introduction to English Literature, vol. v). London (Cresset) 1939; New York (McBride) 1940.

The Story and the Fable. London (Harrap) 1940.

The Scots and their Country. A pamphlet. London (British Council: Longmans) 1946.

Essays on Literature and Society. London (Hogarth) 1949.

An Autobiography. A reprint of *The Story and the Fable*, with some revisions, and seven new chapters. London (Hogarth) 1954.

The Estate of Poetry. Cambridge, Mass. (Harvard University Press) 1962.

3. Articles and Reviews

Muir wrote a very large number of articles and reviews for many periodicals. The following list includes some of the periodicals he wrote for, with the dates between which he was a regular contributor: *European Quarterly*, edd. Muir and Janko Lavrin, 1934–5; *Freeman* (U.S.A.), 1920–4; *Listener*, mostly reviews, 1932–58; *London Mercury*, mostly reviews, 1934–9; *Nation* (U.S.A.), 1924–6; *Nation and Athenaeum*, 1924–9; *New Age*, 1916–24; *New English Weekly*, 1934–5; *Observer*, mostly reviews, 1948–58.

4. Translations by Edwin and Willa Muir

These comprise 43 vols., all but 3 translated from German. Among the most important are:

BROCH, HERMANN: *The Sleepwalkers*, London (Secker) and Boston (Little, Brown) 1932; *The Unknown Quantity*, London (Collins) and New York (Viking) 1935.

KAFKA, FRANZ: *The Castle*, London (Secker) and New York (Knopf) 1930; *The Trial*, London (Gollancz) and New York (Knopf) 1937; *America*, London (Routledge) and Norfolk Conn., (New Directions), 1940.

II. OTHERS

BLACKMUR, R. P.: "Edwin Muir: Between the Tiger's Paws," *Kenyon Review*, XXI (1959), pp. 419–36.

GARDNER, HELEN: *Edwin Muir*, The W. D. Thomas Memorial Lecture, 1961.

GRICE, FRED: "The Poetry of Edwin Muir," *Essays in Criticism*, V (1955), pp. 243–52.

HALL, J. C.: *Edwin Muir*. "Writers and Their Work," No. 71, 1956.

HAMBURGER, MICHAEL: "Edwin Muir," *Encounter*, 87 (1960), pp. 46–53.

HOLLANDER, ROBERT: *A Textual and Bibliographical Study of the Poems of Edwin Muir*, unpublished Columbia University D.Phil. thesis, 1962; also available in the National Library of Scotland.

HOLLOWAY, JOHN: "The Poetry of Edwin Muir," *The Hudson Review*, XIII (1960–1), pp. 550–67.

JENNINGS, ELIZABETH: "Edwin Muir as Poet and Allegorist," *London Magazine*, VII (1960), pp. 43–56.

MILLS, R. J.: "Edwin Muir: A Speech from Darkness Grown," *Accent*, XIX (Winter 1959), pp. 50–70.

RAINE, KATHLEEN: "Edwin Muir: An Appreciation," *Texas Quarterly*, IV (Autumn 1961), pp. 233–45.

STANFORD, DEREK: "Absolute Values in Criticism," *The Month*, 1951, pp. 237–44.

TSCHUMI, RAYMOND: *Thought in Twentieth Century English Poetry*, 1951, Ch. II.